Story List

Introduction

How can I explain my book? One word confusing. This is not the first time this section has been
published. It was published before under the titles
*Climb or Descend: The Ranting of an Ex-Air Traffic
Controller/Bipolar/Suicide Survivor and a Game* and
*I'm Up I'm Down: I'm Bipolar/Suicide Survivor with
a Game.* They were both self-published along with
this one. The first one had sensitive information in it
about my friends, so I republished without it under the
other title. The books had "Episode I" and "Episode
II." "Episode I" was this section and "Episode II" was
a memoir containing journal entries with daily life,
letters, and emails. "Episode II" started off with a
situation at my son's college that could have ended in
a mass shooting using emails. Thank goodness it did
not. I talked about my suicide attempt where I tried
to take the lives of my children with me. Thank God
I changed my mind. It was by getting in a running
SUV and dying from carbon monoxide poisoning in

February of 1996. It took too long. The catalyst for it was after my first delusional hospital stay as "God" on October 27, 1995. I lost my job as an air traffic controller. I lost my identity. It was what I did and was good at it. Now I was thrown into being a stay home mom all the time, and it was boring. I was depressed. I thought I was the only one that could take care of my children properly, so I was going to take them with me. After the suicide attempt and a stay in the hospital, I reinvented myself. I have always been a crafty person, so I sewed a lot and read a lot of romance and suspense novels. In "Episode II," of my other books, I talk about the ups and downs of being bipolar and how I cope with it, my air traffic control experiences (Mostly about my near misses). I work for CVS and give shopping tips (A lot of them are outdated). I talk about my cat Smokey. I had some recipes in it. I must admit it was a little boring. In this part I have a sentence, "Communication in a non-confrontational manner promotes learning." I have always believed in this part of my book, and this is how I am getting information to you in a hopefully non-confrontational manner. My book is made to help people. Make people think on certain subjects and be able to relate to them. Stuff to talk about. I started this part back in August 2009 after my second delusional psychotic hospital stay. On the delusional episodes, I was hospitalized in a lockdown mental illness ward for two episodes. I also had a delusional psychotic experience that my doctor and husband were able to control, so I did not go into the hospital. I started not taking my medication. On the psychotic delusions, I would stay up fixated on something and not get any sleep. They make me believe I have these special powers. The sleep deprivation caused them. I've been diagnosed bipolar since 1997. I will be on mood stabilizers, antipsychotic, and antianxiety medication for the rest of my life. I get so stressed and worked up on something and get manic which is one of the side effects of being bipolar the mood swings. I mostly go manic nowadays. I really do not hit the depression side as much. I have learned to notice the signs of a possible break. They are talking to myself, not eating, pacing around, not sleeping, and drinking too much caffeine. Sometimes throwing my arms around. When I get like this, I take some Ativan for stress, so I calm down, and it helps me get to sleep. I must recognize that I probably cannot do anything to change the situation, so I must figure out ways to cope with it.

The game is quite unusual. I just had this idea, and I went with it. It started out with the stories and poems, but I had this information on the actor, and we had a lot in common, so he went in. This part is still semi-autobiographical. It is fiction and it is nonfiction. The stories really are the important part. Things that might or might not be talked about on a regular basis that could be helpful to people. So, to get the most out of my book read through it the first time then play the game on the second time. I will give you some insight on some of the stories. "The Fun Part," a lot of good information on my book, and what categories to look for which are listed as dedications. "Nothing but the Truth," is the biggest information on me which makes the book nonfiction or semi-autobiographical. It was extremely hard to classify my book this time around. The first two times I classified it as a memoir. This time it is a collector's item with short stories and poems. I put information down in a condensed form. I have these vertical words in my book that tie into the stories. "Wolfie," was my second psychotic hospital stay. "Wolfie," makes you think about anger at children. Yes, they can make you angry, frustrated, and confused. You need to protect them. "Body is not Symmetrical," is a story going after people who do not plan accordingly on trips and then the government must spend money on them to get them out of a difficult situation. "Eve and Adam," is a story to make us realize that the earth has been around for billions of years, and we are doing our best to tear it down. There needs to be an intervention or awareness on our part to protect earth. "Snowball just HIT me," tells one good clue on the actor. It is also about force and how it cannot be the first answer to solving problems. "Thankful," was my hospital stay for my suicide attempt, which I did not tell my husband about. While I was in there this lady opened my eyes at what a lovely family I had, and they were worth living for. "Mother Nature is Hurting," is my nonfiction experience with keeping the earth clean, and it is the first start in saving it. "Survivors vs. Losses," people think that a family member or friend is the survivor in a suicide situation, but that is not true in my opinion. I am a survivor. I chose to continue with life. "My Journal," is an old journal which is nonfiction. "My Letter to Me," is a piece on people who are suicidal to give them time to think about how special they are. "Jonah and the Whale," again keeping the world clean especially water since we cannot live without it. "Obsession," is the catalyst for my first hospitalization which I lost my job and sent me in a downward spiral. "Immaculate Connection," is where I do not believe in Jesus's birth. Drugs can be used in the situation of rape. "Final Destination," do we really know what happens after death mentally? What do we experience? "Distractions," there are so many people having accidents from using cell phones when they are doing something else. Sometimes the accident can result in death. "Mayday! Mayday! Mayday!," another opinion on Jesus's birth which I tie it into air traffic control and a celebrated May occasion. "Destiny," a person's actions can lead up to good or bad destinies or fate. "Addiction," I admit I have a bad addiction to sweets. It is said that a person must reach an exceptionally low point to change. I guess I am waiting for diabetes. "I Have an Idea," I admit I do not know a lot about the government, but there must be a more peaceful way of handling government controlled situations. "Control," things that we can control to make decisions that can be positive or negative. "Lucky," why are there so many people bothering famous people on their personal time? Trying to take a picture of them at their worst time. It seems like the fans are trying to embarrass them. "With or Without You," again the fans are just too into the lives of entertainers, and they fail to give them personal space. Sometimes criminal. "Lost in Translation?" I guess I am going after people who break the law. Especially scammers and hackers. I have fallen for two of them. One I supposedly won money and had to pay taxes on them. The other my computer was frozen, and I paid them in gift cards to release it. By the time I realized it was a scam I had given them $1000 dollars in gift cards. If you must give a gift card for a service or fee, it is probably a scam. If they ask you to give them the activation code on the back, it is pretty much a scam. The scammers can cash the gift cards in. I had to go through the time-consuming process of changing my bank accounts and credit cards. Change all my passwords. "What I Have Learned," things I have learned about myself which might be a good idea for other people to write down too. "I Believe," is what I must believe that life can get better, especially with people. I think a big problem is overpopulation. People having children when they cannot properly take care of them or provide a means of success for their future. I have also put poems in my book. My favorite is "My Stuffed Animal." Children can be so different from their parents, and the parents do not always understand this. So, don't get mad at me and view my book with an open mind.

One thing about this part of my book that makes it different from the other ones is I went more formal on the grammar. For example, I changed a lot of (it's, I'm, and I've) type words to (it is, I am, and I have). It seemed to make my book a better read.

When I was writing this part of my book my favorite editor showed me how to use the internet on how to write something like when to use quotation marks, italicize, hyphens, and other grammatical stuff. A lot of answers I was able to get was to be consistent. When in doubt I capitalized words and used commas. I italicized idioms, slang, and silent thoughts. I hope this explains some of the stuff I have done, and you will not be too confused. Hopefully you will not be too disappointed, and worth the money. So, on with my book.

Dedications

Family and Friends.

To Createspace, without them my book
would not have been published.

To everyone else
I do not want to hurt anyone's feelings
or contradict beliefs. I **respect** the rights
and moral choices of all people.

<u>RESPECT</u>
Right
Endings
Support
People
Everywhere:
Course
Time

P.S. The second time I published this book it was with Outskirts Press, but I left in the first publisher on the dedications for game purposes. Like I said my book would have never been published without Createspace.

Names

In my book I have used some fun names or actor names. A word on actor and actress names—some people looked like them. I have never met these famous people, nor will I force myself on them. I respect their privacy. None of them have been contacted to endorse my book.

Of course, I did use real names on quotations. In history Shakespeare was quoted. Too bad he did not make it in my book. Too confusing and I did not want to wear him out.

A word on the famous (and my favorite) actor I mention. I have never met or seen him in person. Most of the clues were obtained off the internet. My book is about me and not him. It is my thoughts on certain subjects. Remember, all information can be found on the internet or by watching some of his movies. Nothing is new about him that fans cannot find in the privacy of their own homes. I am not spreading rumors—just listing facts.

Shawls

There are loving **shawls** wrapped around my **heart** for these charities. You choose your **lacunas** out of the charities that need the warmth of your love.

SHAWLS

Suicide Prevention: Been there, done that, but not again. It is not the answer, colleagues.

Humane Society: Adopt there.

Alzheimer's: Family member struggled.

World Hunger: Says it all.

Lacunas: Any piece that fits the charity puzzle.

School Fund Razors: Due to budget cuts. You can understand why I used the homophone.

For the letter "L", I didn't know what to use, so I opened my dictionary, and *lo and behold, lacuna: blank space or missing part,* was within three words of *lacrosse.*

Imagine that for a sports nut.

<u>HEART</u>
Health
Enjoyed
At
Right
Time

<u>LACUNAS</u>
Love
At
Countries
Unites
Nations
At
Salutations

Quotations

I use quotations in my book. Since I was unable to get permission for some of them, I will tell you about them and where they might be found. These are my vague versions, but you might get something else out of them. This one by Mahatma Gandhi is on **truth**, **love,** and the **messenger**. It speaks of acceptance, or lack of it, when you deliver information in a certain manner (Thinkexist.com).

<u>TRUTH</u>
Time will
Right and
Unite
The
Human race

<u>LOVE</u>
Lots
Of
Valuable
Energy

<u>MESSENGER</u>
Mankind of
Earth
Sees
Situations
Everyday with
Networking Nations
Good in
Evolution
Right now

The Fun Part

Here is the hitch to get you to buy my book. Because of the controversial subject matter, the shortness of my book, and the little-known fact that I am not famous, I've hidden three dedications for you to find. It's like *Star Wars*. The movies four, five, and six came first. They are family and friends, Createspace, and everyone else.

The third dedication is to music. I love the sound of music, so you will find song titles in my book. There are approximately 343 songs. Most of the great artists are popular today. Songs were especially fun, because I was able to watch the videos and listen to the music at the same time.

The second dedication is to art. I love art. Everything is art in its own individual way. Under art you can find approximately 775 movie, television series, and documentary titles. Again, most of the actors and actresses are popular today, except for the obscure and foreign ones. Some of the titles are easy to recognize. If a sentence is confusing, offensive, or does not read smoothly, it probably has a movie or song in it. Also, I am no expert, and I do not have a college degree. I just have certain thoughts on certain subjects just like everyone else today, so do not take my book too seriously. It's the game you want. You know, you should take it somewhat seriously. I have some very interesting subjects to think about.

I am the ultimate fan. I have paid tribute to over 15 hundred artists in my book. They just do not know it unless they read it. Oh, another thing—this is for all you copyright funny people—I can do this, because they are just everyday words that people use from a dictionary. They are not quotes. It is a thought I am putting in your head. My book makes you think about what people, media, and entertainment have to say about life. Anyway—titles, names, short phrases, expressions, and ideas are not protected by copyright laws.

This is for all you *die-hard fans*, or *true fans*, so to speak. Because of a movie I loved, I was curious, like everyone else, about the actor who was in the movie. The movie was not the famous one he made. I thought, *who is this guy?* So, I researched him from my home on the free internet and found out eight similarities in our lives. This book is dedicated to him because we have common beliefs in anti-war, preserving nature, and it's downright fun. I admire his creativity. I have listed interests, facts about his life, and accomplishments. You can find 31 of his clues surrounded by asterisks throughout my book. When you figure out who he is (due to one obvious physical clue), continue your fun and research him to figure out how all the clues fit in. You will have to be familiar with three of his movies to fit in some of the clues. On IMDb.com, on the mini-biography page, you can put together 19 clues if you look hard. Also, you will find nine of his movies hidden in here, and one song. One of the movies he has a minor part. He has had popular films and in two he was nominated for an Oscar.

Let us play the game of hide-and-seek by finding Blue Eyes, art, and music through the internet. My book is an internet crossword puzzle for your entertainment. Is there another Sherlock Holmes out there?

What a concept! My book is the cutting-edge and innovative phenomenon of suggested camouflage, so have fun with your futuresport. I am going to put on my poker face and *plead the fifth*, so to speak. It is surprising how so many movies and songs are in everyday speech. I am just bringing it to your attention in the form of a book. This technique is stepping outside of the box with writing.

Hopefully, I did not go so overboard on my game that you won't be able to complete it. I guess this is a dare, in a way. You are purchasing, a valuable collectible with my book, because it's the only kind in the world. Act quickly because I think I will be publishing the cheats in the future.

My fellow Americans, every word counts, and there are cheats in the back. Look at my book from start to finish computer wizards. I used YouTube, IMDb, and Netflix for my research, so don't forget about me in all this. You must admit this is a fairly good brainteaser book. Also, you can play for free on the first trial month on Netflix. My book is days of fun or probably weeks maybe even months. You are being informed on the game in this story.

P.S. You can find the creativity of Nicole Kidman, Jason Statham, Sandra Bullock, U2, Coldplay, Will Smith, Kate Winslet, Brad Paisley, Lady Gaga, Adam Lambert, Taylor Swift, and the list goes on and on.

Nothing but the Truth

I want to make a memory not to be forgotten in my research for "Life, Liberty, and the Pursuit of Happiness" (Declaration of Independence), so for the paparazzi I am throwing the truth write out the window of my life. Did you catch the homophone?

1. Family: I have a traditional family. I hope to be the breadwinner with my book of stories, so my husband will get to golf, attend school, cook, and take care of our priceless children. He is a smart man. Turnabout is fair play. Talking about trying your patience with all four activities; therefore, thank you, challenges, for coming to me in the form of children to make the changes in my life. Maybe in the future our family will be able to travel to an island in the sun. Hawaii would be nice, or we could buy the lake house in Georgia. If I cannot have the lake house, a month by the lake would be nice. We could even buy a houseboat.

2. Five foot two and **Eyes of Blue**: I think I am a decent weight for my height and age. It must be that Napoleon Bonaparte blood in me. Rumor has it, somewhere upstream was Napoleon's brother. Some rumors need to be confirmed.

   I have the ultimate gift of being tightly wound. At times, soul stretches, and exercising do me good, but I don't overdo it. No exercising book coming out of me—too many around. I do spend my time cheering on my children in sports and school. It is their time to excel and have the proper love and support they need.

   By the way, it is nice to know I'm related to President Abraham Lincoln by marriage. I have the book to prove it.

   Thank you, James D. Rorabaugh.

3. Friends: I have an abundance of family and friends. It is mostly that Colombian blood on my husband's side of the family. There are enough cards to give me vertigo, and my fingers get numb. If you see me around, and if I have the time form a line—I will try to talk to you. I do not have eyes in the back of my head. If you ask me for my autograph, you will do better if you carry a nice card around that means something to you—or my book. Because there is too much forgery and identity theft going around, I do not

want to see my signature on eBay. I am already **over the half-century mark** and time is of the essence. I like not having the bodyguard around, so I do not need any seriously twisted people. Thank you very much.

4. Throwing Up: When I was an Air Traffic Controller *pushing tin*, so to speak, at LA Center, I would fly in the cockpit for training purposes. I was in the Air Force and received a ride in the phantom jet. It was an F-4 to be specific. Puked my guts out, so you can have those roller coaster rides. A carousel with all the pretty horses is fun for me. Also, no *drunken bouts* for me, and I stay away from the hangover as much as possible. I have had the thrill of a lifetime. I got to fly the fighter too. Oh, yeah!

   H.Y. says, "Hi" to Wichita Mid-Continent Airport and friends in the aviation business. I loved Cessna test pilots. They could do anything for a controller in a bind. Also, I loved working with LA Center area "D" and the facilities bordering it. The pilots were great too. Rest in peace American 11, American 77, United 93, and United 175 who lost their lives on September 11, 2001. You were all great going through LA Center's airspace.

5. Chemical Imbalance: I am Bipolar, and I have accepted it now. I had no control over my illness because it is hereditary. Thank you, Grandma and Aunt. They really suffered back then, when not much was known about the illness. I have fond memories of them—Love you much.

6. Sweets: I am addicted to sugar—pastries, candy. I believe they say it is one of the hardest addictions to overcome.

7. Cats: I love cats. Here is the story. Our evil black cat pounced on a baby rabbit once, and the rabbit squealed for deer life. Here is the thing, I used "deer" because I am against sport killing. I do not think all the animals die a humane death. Of course, I ran over and saved handsome Harry the bunny by getting my predator cat off the cute, defenseless creature. Harry hopped along. No! No! He shot like a bat out of hell on his way, only to be seen eating the flowers the next day. No problem. He was cute to watch.

   About four months later, we think coyotes ate our black cat. Was it karma or survival of the fittest without intervention? Good-Bye **Blackjack**.

   Now we have the cutest Siamese and Tabby-mix cat with the prettiest light blue eyes. We do not let **Calvin** outside except for the upstairs balcony, because he is not a jumper. His adoption was easy from the Humane Society. Calvin had to be put to sleep due to complications from an earlier operation, so I have Smokey now.

CALVIN
Claiming
Adopted pets with
Love increases
Values
In
Nature

8. Cesarean Birth: I was not able to go the nine months due to a stressful job, so my second child wanted to come into this world the opposite way of the recommended procedure. Darn, I did not get an epidural in time. I was too far along, so I was having severe labor pains! Our child is in fetal distress with the cord wrapped around his neck. While the young nurses are wheeling me toward the emergency room, I am repeating in my loudest voice, "Put me out!" I must have scared every expectant mother in there. The birth is a laughable party story for my husband now. My husband was great. Our newborn son was extremely sick afterward, and my husband was able to stay

by our son's side. What teamwork. Our wedding was on Sunday, **October 20th**, 1991.

Another thing about **birth** and postpartum depression. No male is going to say I did not suffer, or they can eat my ballet shoes. Ladies and babies would die in situations like this in the past. I've never passed a gallstone, so I don't know the pain you men have to go through.

BIRTH
Babies
Involve
Routine and
Time for
Health
        Enough said.

9. Hospital: I was hospitalized on 10/27/95 for a chemical imbalance that led to a delusional psychotic episode, due to postpartum depression among other things. Not good when I was writing, "I am God, and I will keep all planes on the ground." I found out later that only the government could make that executive decision.

10. Suicide: I was hospitalized on 02/24/96 for a suicide attempt. I am glad I didn't succeed. I am lucky to be alive. Ten is my favorite number. Around my

old school years, in the town of Waterman, IL. I watched Nadia Comăneci perform the first ten on the uneven parallel bars in the **Olympics**. Pele #10 on the Brazilian soccer team helped his team to three World Cup titles. His bicycle kick is awesome. I am an Olympics fan and a **soccer fan**. "Yeah!" Also, Kerri Walsh and Misty May are great for 3 Olympic gold medals back-to-back in beach volleyball. You go girls! These high achievers gave me something to strive for at being a mom. Suicide is a red-flag illness and cannot be ignored. Check yourself into a **hospital** like I did. There are several avenues for help.

HOSPITAL
Health
Of
Some
People
Include
Time and
Awareness using
Love

There it is in a nutshell. You will find me with no make-up, in sweats, t-shirts, caps, and old jeans. I like to be comfortable, and I do have bad hair days. Just being normal and past the bikini-beach part of life.

I try to keep events positive in my life now. U Smile.

Signed,
P.J. Henry

Wolfie

This is the **story**.

<u>STORY</u>
Schedule time
Together with
Older
Relatives
You all

When I was in the hospital on 08/20/09 for my second delusional episode, I was a witness to an incident between a nurse and a patient who was on some serious medication. This patient was so bad that she was swaying with slurred speech and shaky hands. I even volunteered to push the lady, Jane Doe (not her real name), around in a wheelchair for the day. This nurse in her harshest voice says, "The situation is under control," and tells me not to worry. Later in the day the nurse was trying to get the patient to wake up and eat. Because the nurse was forcing food down the lady's throat, I thought the patient would choke.

I have been on medication like that before. On my first visit to the hospital on 10/27/95 for mental illness, I was given so much medication that I did not know what the nurses did to me. I found out the next day that a staff member came into my room in the early evening to take me to X-ray. The roommate I had told me what happened.

On with the "Wolfie" story.

The lunchroom incident almost put *the last straw on the camel's back*, so to speak, because I thought she was mean. My emotions were boiling. I almost let the nurse have it, but I do not have a history of violence. I had to leave the lunchroom in tears, because I could not do anything physical to improve the situation. One of the other nurses saw me crying and explained the situation. That made me stop crying, but after the understanding nurse left, I got mad again.

I got so mad, that I started hitting a stuffed wolf that I called Wolfie. I won the stuffed wolf in the facility auction. This auction is great. Patients bid on new items that people donate like stuffed animals, men's and women's clothes, knick-knacks, jewelry, and snacks. All were inexpensive items. The bucks were little white pieces of paper with a dollar bill printed on it. We would earn the bucks by attending therapy groups at the hospital. There were about five groups a day. My two favorites were arts & crafts and psychology.

A friend of mine, whom I will nickname Dances with Wolves, saw me beating up Wolfie because I was mad. Because Dances with Wolves, loved wolves so much, she took Wolfie away to what she called Wolf Protective Services, until I calmed down. I finally got Wolfie back like my friend promised.

I know child abuse happens, but it is time to stop the abuse now. I was taking my anger, frustration, and confusion out on my child at the time. Wolfie was there for comfort, not a punching bag. I could have always given my child to relatives or Child Protective Services.

I am persuading you with children to look at the good qualities and not the bad.

P.S. The nurse did change her attitude toward patients because she received a lecture from her supervisor. The nurse was quite nice after that, and I asked her to be my discharge nurse. Everyone has a bad day occasionally. I am just trying to persuade you to not let it affect other people.

Body is not Symmetrical

Roll a pitch black ball on an inclined flat top surface above the floor. After the symmetrical ball goes in a straight line and falls off the table for three, it dies.

Now, roll a two-headed dime on a flat surface. The outcome will always be the same. The coin loses energy and always falls heads-up. That is why they don't use two-headed coins in sports. It is like *stacking the deck*, so to speak.

I heard once that the human body is not symmetrical. One side is stronger than the other, so that is why we go in circles.

Here is the theory. I go out in a **sandstorm in the desert** with no **water** and find out I go in circles. While I was looking at my left foot, I think I go right. It is hard to tell with the sand blowing. My right side is more developed, because I kick soccer balls, write, and hit volleyballs better with it. I am young at heart, and you would think of me as a jock in my younger years. Because I am right-side dominant, my right leg pulls more; therefore, my circle goes right. I favor the right side because I am not ambidextrous. Because the sun is too hot, I do not travel in the day. Remember the sand is blowing, so I cannot follow the stars home. I get lost and nobody is around to help me. I am praying to the desert saints to get me out. Also, I am saying the "F" word a lot, but it's not helping.

It would have been nice to *stack the deck*, so to speak in my favor by having Girl or Boy Scout training, going to a sports store, or checking on the internet for tips and proper equipment for the hiking trip. I should have brought some **friends**, so I would not get lonely. You know, *a friend in need is a friend indeed*, so to speak. Now they must send a helicopter after me, and they find my body *blowin'* in the wind.

<u>FRIENDS</u>
Funny
Rapport
Intelligent
Encouraging
Nice
Dependable
Safe

I know this story is a little farfetched, but the scenario does happen. I will be safe the next time I hike. I am curious because people know something is wrong, and they do not do anything about it. I am informing you that activities don't always go your way. With better planning and research this will provide a more pleasant outcome.

Eve and Adam

Remember, I respect other people's beliefs. I just want to make people think about myths, legends, and the possibilities of saving lives.

Part of the legend goes like this: There was, supposedly, in the past, a man called Adam when there was no written word. There was gossip by 12 monkeys in the Garden of Eden. I do not think animals could write back then. There was no one to teach them new tricks.

Adam wanted to increase the human species, and he was fearless, so he took one of his ribs and made a female named Eve. Eve could talk, and she gossiped about an anaconda named Hancock. Eve fell out of **grace** with the enchanted Garden of Eden. Adam had to follow so he could spread his DNA.

GRACE

Good cook
Righteous
Always there
Clever
Extraordinary

(I had to stick in Mother-in-Law's name.)

Sorry, I cannot believe Adam and Eve legend. No cloning back then. Also, no sterile utensils to use. This is how the story could have happened between Eve and Adam. You know ladies come first. This is one of my favorite stories.

Now this story is all about Eve and her sisters. In the land that time forgot, there were lady frogs named Eve. They could have babies on their own, without male sperm, because they had a special atom in their bodies. The Eves had about 300 eggs each that turned into tadpoles. The Eves named the boy ones Jack, and the girl ones Christine.

After the eggs hatched, the tadpoles developed red tails and could swim underwater for an exceptionally long time. Some tadpoles got curious to go on land, so they developed legs and hopped around like mom. Other tadpoles liked to stay in the water, so they developed into fish. Some of the big fish got really big.

The land frogs could only just breathe air in the process of creation. Some of the air-breathing frogs liked the history of where they came from in the water, so some would have babies in the water. Others liked to have their babies on land, but the frogs that stayed on land developed hard eggs. The land frogs grew bigger and bigger. Some of the frogs liked hopping around so much that they grew feathers and became birds. There it is, folks, the egg came first. All these processes took an exceedingly long time. Now some of the birds decided to fly. Some of the land frog's eggs on the ground hatched into reptiles. The ground reptiles could go fast to catch food. Both animals continued to have eggs. Some of the reptiles got really, really big and called themselves dinosaurs. Some of the reptiles stayed small.

Now this is where the alternate endings start.

Well, I should go beginnings first. In the beginning, aliens could have started the evolution process. Nah. More believable is from tiny, tiny organisms, but I did not like the fish part due to scales. See, frogs could have come from fish. OK, back to the alternate endings.

I will talk about the dinosaurs first. There were some dinosaurs that got really big, but some stayed small to bury themselves under the ground. The ground ones survived this big snow, because it was warm in their underworld. Some went into hibernation or ate their brothers to survive. The big dinosaurs died during the ice age because there were no clothes back then.

After a long, long time some of the small reptiles developed fur to stay warm, so the furry ones started to go up on the cool surface to eat food. Some of the fury animals liked staying the same, but some liked hanging from trees and developed tails.

Oh, I forgot, once the furry animals came along, they kept the eggs inside of them, because they loved the eggs so much.

Now back to the story. The ones that liked their tails named themselves monkeys. Now some of the monkeys liked to stay on the ground, so they lost their tails and called themselves apes. The apes on the ground split again. Some stayed apes, but the others became the missing link. Now some of the missing link's bodies went so far down in the earth that their bodies burned up. Where does volcano lava come from?

Now, with the planet of the apes, Neanderthal man came along after a long, long time. Now, Neanderthal man started to develop into caveman. Man started to lose more fur, and they became different colors depending on where they could find food. Some went to warm climates and some to cold ones. All man developed so they could wear clothes, speak, read, write, and build things with their hands.

This story goes along with compost and the development of the earth and how vegetation grew. Water came from the snow, which could have covered the earth at one time. It is just a story.

Here is the bird scenario. The birds that could fly liked to fly and developed excellent eyesight to find food. Some birds stayed on the ground, so they developed bad eyesight and decided to eat seeds and bugs.

I know this story is long, but this splitting stuff takes a long, long time, like millions and billions of years. Also, all these animals developed different DNA.

Oh, forgetful me. It must be the lost bytes again. In the beginning, the frozen earth could have been so far away from the sun that the earth had snow all over it. The moon decided it liked the earth so much, that it hit and drove the earth close to the sun and made most of the snow melt. The new moon decided to hang around because it loved the earth so much. This action created the solar system in which we live. OK, I am no expert, but who really knows how the universe works?

OK, my computer is working again, so on with the bird story.

Some of the birds on the ground lost their feathers and turned into monkeys. The monkeys split. Okay, my fingers are getting sore, so go back to the split between monkeys and apes. In the legend, man decided to tell the shortened story of Eve and Adam. Not enough paper and quills back then.

It's a mad, mad, mad, mad world. Now man keeps killing each other and destroying the earth with war, violence, overpopulation, and pollution. Sometimes the situations listed can be prevented a little, but someday, if this does not change, man shall become extinct sooner rather than later. Humans exercise instead of playing with your toy guns and bombs. Anyway, who thinks that they can rule the world?

I believe in The Big Bang Theory about earth and over billions of years developed life. Earth could not have developed in six days, seven nights, but I might believe man will destroy it in six days. What will it take to end all wars?

Nobody is perfect. Because I am only human, I make mistakes too, but I try not to, now. With this story I am trying to persuade you to take an active part in saving it.

P.S. Atoms should not be used for bombs and wargames.

Snowball just HIT me

When we were young, I took a snowball in the **face** when I was about **eleven**. The snowball had little pebbles in it; consequently, I received a tiny **scar on the lip**. It was the lower one. I leaped on my older brother. Because of the girl thing, he held me down till I calmed down.

I was just a kid then, but now I know I managed the situation badly. It can be that sibling rivalry sometimes.

FACE
Force
Always
Challenges
Everyone

The way I handled it was a negative way of solving my pain. I should have gone inside and splash water on my funny face, but when I calmed down, this cry-baby went to mom. Of course, she cleaned me up, but she saw the fight. She says, I must pay with consequences for my actions. She grounded me. That already happened with my brother. She made me do the right thing. I had to apologize to my brother for the **force** I used.

FORCE
Finding
Ordeals and
Rages can
Control
Earth's plan

He mentioned something about it being all right. What a sport. Learned a lesson about dirt-clod fights that day. Did you say, dirt-clod? Yes, it was a beautiful day in the summer. The fighting was for a dirt-clod fight, but I could not fit the "S" in. "SHIT," I confessed and got a mouth full of dirt too.

We are young every day of our lives, because on the day you wake up, you will be waking up to the unknown. What is going to happen today? Will I make a mistake? Will I have a positive outlook on life? Will someone else make a mistake that will affect my life? Will I make it through the day? What will the future hold? Will I do something I will regret? Will I learn something new? Will someone do something for me out of the kindness of his or her heart? Do you know if you will make it through the day? More senseless mass shootings. Do I have to prepare for death? Do I wake up and say somebody might kill me? Where I go today, will it be safe? I would like to know my day of departure. This does not include suicide. Make it so someone knows enough about my computer to close out all my accounts and get my bills in order. Someone to contact everybody in my phone and contact lists about my death.

Have a nice day.

Art

Everyone is a masterpiece of art in his or her own individual way. It is just that I might not understand the message the person is trying to bring to life.

I love the **earth**. It has the word **art** in it. The primary colors that create all colors are yellow, **blue, and red**. I learned that information while volunteering for Art Corps at my children's school. You will find these colors in **Venezuela**, Colombia, and Ecuador flags.

Everyone has his or her favorite artworks. Be it his and hers, nature, or someone else's. For instance, my favorite artist is Bev Doolittle. She paints in camouflage associated with spiritual aspects some of the times. **"Pintos"** rocketed her to stardom. "Bugged Bear" is my favorite, because it reminds me of being a mom resting from a hectic schedule as it flies around me. Parents are the first teachers in a child's life. Parents mold children to make positive decisions.

EARTH
Everyone's
Average
Rage is
Tough on
Humanity

ART
Always
Right
Timing

P.S. Using a **camera** why is earth's **picture** fading?

Thankful

I went into the hospital after a suicide attempt. I was on a lost highway with a point of no return. What I did was go into our garaged running SUV with my children and family dog. My husband was away on a business trip. I did not realize it, but I was sick. I had lost my job as an air traffic controller because of a delusional psychotic episode after the birth of my second child. I was forced to stay home with my children. I thought my life from then on would be boring and hopeless. I lost my energy and creativity. I had never planned to stay home with children like my mom. I did not have a gun at the time. I always wonder if I would have succeeded if I did. Well, the plan did not work. It took too long. After that I checked myself into a hospital because I was afraid, I might try again. My husband only knew I was going into the hospital for suicidal thoughts. I did not tell him about the attempt.

I met up with another lady, and she helped me

realize I had a lot to be thankful for in my life. She was asking me questions like if I was homeless, abused, or a drug addict. My answers were "No." My family came to visit, and she said to me they were beautiful. I was caught up in my own misery and not thinking of the others in my life. I was suffering from losing a job I dearly loved. She was sent there to talk to my heart and soul. The police brought her in. The police really do have our well-being in mind. Play fairly and let the police do their job to serve and protect.

After I got out, I reinvented myself. I made myself get busy. I enrolled my children in preschool activities. I started sewing and needle point. I started reading romance novels which was not the best subject matter, but it kept my mind active.

My thoughts, do you need a suicide note to family or friends? They will think it was their fault anyway or did not do enough to prevent it. I know I did not. I sent a picture of me and the kids to my mom with our birthdates on it. Later in life Robin William's starred in the movie, *What Dreams May Come.* I wonder if that movie was around before my life challenge, would it have made a difference? I think about that movie a lot. Would I have gone to an undesirable place? I would have taken a life. So, you should tell them how you feel beforehand, to help you with a positive decision to live. They might be able to help. They will hurt for a long time-possibly forever. Go into a hospital, you will never know unless you try to change. Talk to someone. The National Suicide Prevention Lifeline is 800-273-8255. It is confidential. Try looking up suicide pictures on the internet and see what you will look like when you leave this wonderful world. They are not pretty. Remember though, you just might not succeed. Then what? You could do some severe damage from which you cannot recover. It could involve other people's lives. Losing your mobility is an especially important subject matter to consider if you fail.

P.S. In my original books I had this section as suicidal thoughts, but I decided to go into more detail this time around.

Mother Nature is Hurting

I am going to tell a powerful story in God's country. I was walking through the park one fine day in the merry, merry month of August. I was walking to my son's new school to see about a schedule change, because school would be starting in two weeks. This is a sparkling new school with hope for a better future for our growing students. This school is so planned out that the students get to rent laptops to take home for homework. It is nice. The office was closed. I did not reach the goal of a schedule change, but I received something else. I was walking tall, home at a leisurely pace, and saw trash on the school grounds.

Once upon a time, there was a lost plastic water bottle that I found. I said to myself, *somebody who was reckless needs this bottle*, so I picked it up while going my way home. Next was the cup, someone had used and lost it too. I picked up the cup and, *lo and behold*, I saw more valuable items. Now, this took at least fifteen minutes to pick up the valuable items. I was bending over a lot and got a good workout. These people's backs must have been hurting to not accomplish such an easy job.

Then some people left little bags of poop around the sidewalk area. I thought how considerate of these people to leave these bags of poop. At least they put their valuable items in a bag.

Now my cup *runneth* over, and my two hands are full. I was still hopeful to find the owners. I passed several people on my way home. They did not seem to want the items, so I kept on walking. Luckily, the American poop had stopped because these certain people got to an open street area. They can be shy.

Who are these people who think they are so good? I did not see the people who left the trash along my walk. Surely, they would not throw such valuable objects out the window of their cars.

I came home realizing, I could not find the owners, so I put the heavy items in a safe place. I think responsible humans would put these items in a recycle container and trashcan. After I put the items in a safe place, I went inside to wash my hands. While I was washing my hands, I was thinking, *I just performed surgery on Mother Nature's cancer.* I could not get it all, so she is dying now. I wonder if I will get a cap and gown for my energy.

We are the world, and we have the **power of now** to change. The planet is getting hotter. The glaciers are melting. The vanishing forests are not helping. Trash is building at a phenomenal rate. Please protect our natural resources before it is too late.

POWER of NOW
Participation in
Obstacles
Would
End
Right
of (In the)
Notebook
Of
Wonder

P.S. I'm married to Mother Nature, and she isn't happy. This story is to persuade you to keeping the earth clean.

Survivors vs. Losses

This is a serious subject again, but it's always on my mind. This is a messy subject. People think of all kinds of ways to end their **lives**. This hurts the loved ones when these dazed and confused people succeed. One person jumped off the bridge in San Diego to evade the police, but the police dog that was attempting to subdue him died. This incident has been accepted.

<u>LIVES</u>
Lives
Include
Valuable
Energy for
Survival

The police dog takes months of training, and it hurts the police officer very much to lose a partner, be it the animal or human. I would like to include American firefighters in this pain, and all who lose a lovely and amazing person. Suicides hurt the ones they leave behind.

Let us talk about survivors. I have heard of people surviving big bear attacks, a shark attack, cancer, plane crashes etc., but what about the person who has serious suicidal thoughts, or tries to accomplish the deed and finds the answers to go on living? They who have tried are the real **suicide** survivors. It is the relatives or friends who must go through the loss of family or friends. The loss means you have cared very much and could not help.

<u>SUICIDE</u>
Survivors
Under
Intense
Challenges should
Include
Decisions
Equal to life

I am a suicide survivor because I had to be hospitalized to seek help. There are some people who went through the physical pain of self-infliction. I am thinking that the real survivor is the person who wants to end all the pain in their life but realizes they can go on with life's unexpected challenges. The loved one must accept loss and go on with life.

P.S. Suicide survivors, it is somewhere only we know. Just say yes to life.

My Journal

Here are some old journal entries. The grammar is not perfect in my journal entries, and there are fragmented sentences. The first entry is a letter I wrote to my brothers and sister. My ex-husband and I get along fine now since we realized we needed a divorce. (Well maybe not with the publishing of my book.)

February 2003.

Well, I lost it last night. I spent almost the entire evening crying. Think how it would be if almost daily you had someone pointing out your faults: the house isn't clean enough, watch too much TV, fat belly, hair is too dark and curly, very sedentary, cooking is not desirable, and saying digs all the time to you just loud enough for you to hear and no one else. Well, that is what my husband has been doing to me. He has hurt me terribly.

Last night, I made a great dinner for his aunt and her husband. They came over to watch a movie, and it was long. Here it is 10:30pm, and I get the kids ready for bed because of school the next day. My son is hungry, so he fixes a cheese sandwich and takes his time eating. My husband comes in and raises his voice at our son to "Hurry up," but before he goes, he tells me not to make brownies anymore. I made them for dessert. He says, "It makes me mad to see you make a pig out of yourself in front of my family." I'm almost in tears after that comment and then when he comes in again, he yells at our son. I told him, "Just leave him alone." He says he can't then he goes away. It was his idea to show the long movie on a school night. Then I started crying and stayed in the kitchen to clean up.

In the past, what differences we have had, we have kept from the kids. Not this time. Our son asks whom will I pick if we get a divorce. I told him I would get both him and his sister and not to worry. I have been civil to him. I do not cut him down like he does me. He gave me roses and a card Monday morning for Valentine's Day and apologizes for the way he has been acting. We had a talk Wednesday night about him losing his temper with the kids too much. I told him that night about his digging comments, and he said they were all true. I don't watch as much TV as he thinks. Yes, I will sew and watch HGTV for home decorating ideas, but I don't watch soaps.

He came home very early last week two nights without calling me and sneaked in. He later admitted he wanted to catch me at doing nothing. We have been at odds lately on getting the kids to do things. He seems to push too much and not let the kids be kids. He is pushing the kids and me away. What does he want? Is he jealous of me because I stay home with the kids? He commented that he was hurt that I did not call him on Valentines or give him a card. I didn't think he deserves one. Also, I could not think of an appropriate gift. He thinks he can buy roses, and everything will be alright. I'm starting to realize I married a cruel and judgmental man. I call mom. She works so she can get away from the criticizing dad does to her.

My husband is going to be one of those grumpy old men that takes life out on other people. He says he feels "stagnant, trapped, and hopeless." He finally realized I'm not the person he married. I'm realizing he is not the man I married. He puts a lot of stress on himself because he wants to keep up appearances. I'm thankful that my family and I are healthy. I love my kids. I have lost respect for him now, and I know he has with me by the way he treats me.

He does not see the good in the morning and being able to love people for who they are. He wants to control us. He admits he is a terrible teacher, and that is what a parent is. He is getting a lot of stress from the houses, and I can't convince him to sell this one. I would love to have the new house. It is bigger, so we could stay away from each other more easily in it. In ten years, our daughter will be going off to college. Hopefully she will be on a scholarship of some sort. What will my husband and I have in common? We will not stay married if he keeps up this hurting way he has.

I'm going to see Dr. Z, my psychiatrist, next week. Maybe my husband is so depressed that he needs to go on medication. He needs to find answers and peace of mind.

Pray for understanding. I have made these choices on information I had and the person I was in the past. I will live with them, but I can make choices for the future to keep a smile on my face and the shining sun on it even when it rains. Life is too short to have someone harping on you.

(I have gone back and forth about putting this letter in here, but my book is part memoir/biography, in a way. The ugly truth needs to come out at times.)

This next sequence contains questions the kids have asked me through the years.

Mom, can you teach me to read?
Mom, I wonder why flowers grow?

Mom, can I become an artist?

Mom, how do you know all the answers to my questions?

Mom, why do birds fly, and we do not?

Mom, can I have some candy?

Mom, why does dad go to work?

Mom, why do people litter?

Mom, why am I here?

Mom, why are the beautiful stars so far away?

Mom, why does music sound so sweet?

Mom, why is my kitty soft?

Mom, why does my kitty purr?

Mom, can you make me a Halloween costume? (I love sewing **Halloween** costumes.)

Mom, can I play in the rain?

Mom, can you push me on the swing?

(Mom was my first teacher.)

December 3, 2005.

Today I went to volunteer at the Humane Society and found some dogs there that touched my heart. One's name was Peggy. Her front paw was deformed from birth, but she had a heart with signs of a real enthusiastic future. There was another dog that wanted to get to know me. It had one blue eye and one brown eye. There was a deaf Dalmatian. I could talk to it in a way. I motioned with my hand for it to come over and it did. It was one of the special needs dogs, so I couldn't walk it. I probably would have taken it home if I had.

12/04/05.

Yellow Daffodils are my favorite flower for as long as I can remember. They are grown from bulbs and bloom in the spring. The yellow Daffodil for me symbolizes freedom of affection. They are so vibrant and cheery. They take me out of my depressive moods. I wonder who thought up their name. How long have they been around? It is a nice day out for December.

12/07/05.

I would like to see Bev Doolittle this Sunday. She has spiritual meaning to her art. I ran across a mother who died of cancer, Marjorie Williams, on the net. She was a columnist, and her husband got together her columns and essays, and had them printed after her death. I would like to read her book, *The Women at the Washington Zoo-Writings on Politics, Family, and Fate.*

12/08/05.

I dreamed about a big earthquake and rainstorm last night. I was in a house looking outside at the stormy weather. I was not feeling the earthquake, but cracks started forming on the walls and got bigger and bigger. There was no grass, just dirt. Off in the distance is a flat mountain of rock, and it crumbles down. Then there are blue skies, nobody else around that I could see, but I start hearing them after the earthquake. Nothing happens to me.

I raced last night, but it was controlled. I keep getting ideas for books, poetry, drawings, photography, screenplays, but I do nothing about it. I feel a need to simplify my life. It seems that there is too much to remember. I know now that my family comes first. How could I have thought of suicide? I must not say or do anything in haste.

12/10/05.

This day flew by. The most memorable time today was when the Christmas tree fell down. I went to the Humane Society again. The deaf Dalmatian was still there. No sign of the other two dogs. We went and picked out the tree as a family and decorated it. It was so nice. I don't remember decorating it together in the past. Usually, I decorate it by myself. I wonder what my son will say when he sees it missing after this Christmas. I made a good fish dinner tonight. I didn't get around to drawing or poetry today. I'm thinking of taking a job cleaning out stables. The nice part is the free riding lessons. I might not be able to start until after the New Year though.

12/11/05.

My son and I did some weeding around the house, and his dad was very proud of him. Our softball team won tonight, and it was great. We were one lady down, so we had to take an out when the ghost came up. We named her Lucky. I would like to read, John Milton's *Paradise Lost*.

12/12/05.

Wow! I had a big crying day in the morning, but I took a shower and felt better. Character, what is it and who defines it in a person? If I don't do something I say I will, is that a mark on my character? If I'm always an hour late for events, is that bad character? If I can't survive a marriage, is that bad character? If I'm more of a seeker, is that good character? Is it just fantasizing about what I have or have not learned in life? I wonder what I will be doing on this day in 2012.

12/17/05.

I really messed up my pinkie finger today playing softball. I slid into second base with my right hand first and it jammed my finger. I fractured the bone, dislocated it, and pulled a tendon. One of the players had to take me to urgent care. Because my finger swelled, my friend had to cut off the ring on that finger.

12/23/05.

A list of my favorite movies and why I like them:

Phantom of the Opera, 2004: Music and clothes were great, but it is about a lady torn between good and evil in some way.

Mindwalk, 1990: A scientist, politician, and poet/writer happen to get together and talk about their certain fields of interest. Nothing is solved except more understanding from different points of view. It makes you think.

Powder, 1995: A flour white boy with no hair is found after his grandpa dies. The boy is off the charts in I.Q. He is afraid of lightning. Everyone is harassing him, and he can't understand why they are cruel to him. He turns into pure energy at the end.

Hidalgo, 2004: The movie reminds me of Bev Doolittle's artwork and how spiritual she is with nature. Some of her work is camouflage. Too bad I wasn't around horses more.

Pride and Prejudice, 2005: The wardrobe and music were great. You got to agree Matthew MacFadyen is such a *hottie*.

12/24/05.

Our Christmas Eve Novena. This one is for the family. At midnight the kids open their presents from his side of the family. I don't want an Xbox 360 right now. They are too high in demand. The Xbox is my husband's Christmas present. He needs something to show for his life, and I understand. He feels like he is not appreciated. Oh, one of the prices of being human and not spiritual. This has been a very sunny day. May our Christmas be merry and bright tomorrow? I'm looking forward to the holiday.

12/25/05.

Christmas morning! Wow! How quiet it is right now. Blackjack playing around woke me up, so I put the presents under the tree from my side of the family. We will go to Tia's house for hot chocolate and homemade bread. Living life in the present makes you happy.

12/26/05.

A lot of clean-up today. Still not done. The kids are disagreeing over Play Station time. It seems like a lot of stuff in the house is pulling the family apart, so materialistic. Why do I have a hard time getting them into more reading and writing? Creativity and activity. They seem to be cruel to Blackjack at times, but I know it's them forcing attention on him.

12/27/05.

Good morning. I think I'm falling out of my manic stage. Right now, easy answer, just relaxing. Am I dependent on this family or is the family dependent on me? It's a wonderful life I have. It's complicated right now. I'm looking to simplify my life right now in my own way. Not by forces. Evil produces misery. Good actions result in happiness. Evil compares to poisoned honey. It's tempting but laden with death. Overcoming restlessness of body and mind by concentration techniques has achieved astonishing results. I took a nice long bath today. It was relaxing, massaging my body and soaking the tension away. Why did it give me a headache?

12/28/05.

I thought about Cindy Sheehan and her son dying in Iraq. That's a deep loss when your child dies. We should try talking to the students in High School and suggest alternatives to joining the Armed Forces. War can be stopped, just convince people not to join. Why raise children to go to war? It's the freedom we are fighting for. I went to the gym today and a walk with my husband to Lake Hodges. I wanted to sit and reflect. He wanted to move. What have I shown for this year? Art and math classes. Trying to learn keyboard and guitar. Do I have to show something for my life or is just being a good person enough? Do I just exist, or do I help with changes in the world? How can I teach my children not to get caught up in all the material things of this planet?

12/29/05.

Is life a tragedy that I have chosen to be part of? The best way to learn is from other people's mistakes. The point I'm getting at is, I don't know who to give credit for my life. Did I bring myself down here or did I come against my will? I guess it's got something to do with heaven and hell on earth. Why would I come back?

12/30/05.

I don't understand again. I've been confused. One has to hide so others can seek. Why do I write? I took the pills. It has been a cold December. (Due to my illness, I do things that I would normally not do. I think I was trying to simplify too much and threw out my other journals. This is it for 2005.)

September 27, 2009.

(This starts one of my journals that I started after I got out of the hospital over Labor Day. There is a lot of time to write, when I was in the hospital on my "Deborah the Prophetess" phase. What made this psychotic experience unique was I was not talking to anyone. I was writing everything down. I thought they could not hear me.)

My daughter's team won at volleyball the other day. She still isn't talking to me much. I think it was my crying meltdown about Calvin escaping, door, and the way they treat me. The anniversary of my first breakdown is coming up in a month 10/27/95. "I am God," funny me.

October 2, 2009.

I pulled out a pay stub from my husband to show my divorce lawyer. It had the date 09/11/09. This was a random act. Is it a sign on the divorce proceedings? The lawyer I have is funny, and I like him.

10/03/09.

Since our children are old enough to stay home alone now, we are going to tell the kids about the divorce tomorrow. We waited years for the divorce. In the bedroom downstairs is where I'm staying since I got back from the hospital.

10/04/09.

We told the kids we're getting a divorce. The kids are alright with it. My daughter knew it was coming. My son didn't have a clue, but he took it well. I was the only one that cried. I love my kids very much. I'll be there for you kids, always. Let's go on with my book.

10/08/09.

I watched **Lord of the Rings** today. I got the idea for "Precious." Life, Soul, Senses, Time, and

Wonder are precious, not an object like a ring. I got the idea for "Circle of Friends." Circle meaning ring and friends meaning fellowship. Match my poem to J.R.R. Tolkien talking about the ring and how it affects the people it comes in contact within his book, *The Fellowship of the Ring*. If you are not familiar with the story, I'm hearing, "Them all," "Them all," but I'm thinking "The mall," "The mall." (This sentence may not make sense, because I was not able to use his quotation.) While I was watching the movie, I was writing down all the words that they mentioned from my book. There are a lot.

10/10/09.

I wonder what it all will mean a year from now, 10/10/10. Ten is my favorite number.

10/13/09.

I'm starting to race on movies. I watched several movies and wrote down the words that are in the movie that are in my book. What does it mean? Everything happens for a reason.

10/15/09.

I got together a bunch of stuff for the facility auction where I stayed for two weeks. I did a good job. A lot of the stuff is new that was sitting around the house. I got one of my neighbors to donate some stuff too. (I was going through my old journals from my hospital stay on 08/20/09 and found this note that someone had written to me while we were there. She didn't put her name on it, and I can't remember her name.)

Peggy Sue,

"You have been a joy in my life at the amount of time I've known you. Thank you for your encouragement and sincerity. You are one of those God sent people in my life. Good luck in your journey and your book.

Someday when I go to a bookstore I'm going to say, Hey! I know Peggy Sue! I love U. God Bless."

(You make friends when you are in the hospital, which I called the *safe house*. It was co-ed, so the guys slept on one side and ladies on the other. You feel for the people who have tried to commit suicide or are thinking about it. There are a lot of people who don't have a place to go after their stay. I went in as "Deborah the Prophetess." I wasn't talking to anybody. I was just writing everything down. I thought no one could hear me, but they could read. I was really into the Bible for some reason and giving advice on life. I think I chose "Deborah" because I always loved the name "Debbie" growing up. My friend was calling me Peggy Sue.)

10/16/09.

I found it. The book a friend told me about. This book is great. It tells you how to get published. The friend was in the hospital with me. There is a reason why we meet people at a certain time in our lives. I would've never found the book if it wasn't for her. I went to the hospital to drop off the auction stuff. It was nice to see some of the staff again.

10/21/09.

Hello new journal. You will get to know all of my secrets. I'm only going to use red ink in you. I'm really partial to the color red lately. The kids and I went down to Balboa Park and Zoo. We had a good time. We live in the City of San Diego, and it is beautiful. My daughter is taking driving lessons.

10/26/09.

I got it! I was listening to a song on the radio, and I happened to find it in my book. I started to look up other songs and movies. There are a lot of titles in everyday language. I needed this. Who is going to want to read a book about someone like me? I still don't know what to call it.

10/27/09.

Well, this is the anniversary of my first breakdown, where I was writing down, "I am God." So much time has passed by. My daughter asked me to get something for her today. I said, "You have two perfectly good legs." She said, "OK." Sometimes it's that simple.

10/28/09.

I'm feeling good today. I have holes on my toes that match my moles. I just finished reading *Renegade: The Making of a President*, by Richard Wolffe on President Obama. Good book.

10/30/09.

Well, I made it to Illinois without any delays. The airplane ride was smooth on the way over. I'm here to see Mom. I made up a poem on the plane, "Starlight." I took my luggage on the plane, so I didn't have to go through the baggage claim.

10/31/09.

What a day. It was hard seeing mother. She had a good day, and it was very cold. We went to see the old house where I got my scar. This might be the last time I get to see my mother. I love you, Mom. As I lay me down to sleep, I read a book that makes me weep, then I count the people I meet. Why do I cry so much at happy endings? It must be menopause. I miss celebrating Halloween with my children.

Sweet November 3, 2009.

Another sunny day in San Diego, and it's good to be back.

11/05/09.

Good day today. To manic or not to manic? That is the question. Now that makes sense. I don't think I will be able to write another book. Maybe I can publish the cheats in the future? It would be nice for the artists to know who they are.

11/08/09.

It was mom's birthday today. It was a shock to see her last weekend. If I saw her again, she probably wouldn't remember me.

11/09/09.

I read over my book and found some editing mistakes. Will I ever be done? I went to the movies with my friend, and I told her everything is fine with the divorce. She was concerned.

11/16/09.

I started a cheat sheet for my book. A publisher has to buy this idea. I wrote "The Quatrain" today. It tells my future. The Nostradamus book I have been reading was the inspiration.

11/17/09.

I made up "Creativity" today. It's pretty short, but it hits the point. My life is a resumé. Does your life make you who you are? Do you ever wonder what it would be like in someone else's shoes? Would you be that person or who you are now?

11/18/09.

I came up with "Eternity" today.

11/21/09.

I made a new friend today. She lives across the street, and she is going through a real messy divorce. I'm glad mine is amicable. Hopefully, I can help her in the future.

11/24/09.

I made up "Hummingbird" today. It is dedicated to the end of **Hidalgo**. (Remember when Frank sets Hidalgo free in the end.) I don't think you can keep hummingbird's captive. They are the only bird that can fly backward. No wonder you can't cage them. They don't have a rear-view mirror.

December 1, 2009.

There is a Blue Moon this month. That is when there are two full moons in a month. I have a Blue Moon birthday. I call it that when my birthday lands on Mother's Day; therefore, my zodiac sign is Taurus. I don't like to get birthday presents anymore, except when my Blue Moon birthday comes around.

12/12/09.

OMG! I love to watch rugby. It is so brutal with all the pushing and non-stop action. I wonder what I will be doing on 12/12/12.

12/19/09.

I will be moving back to the old house after school is out. I guess it was a good idea to keep it after all. The renters have been good.

12/20/09.

Thinking about Blue Eyes today. Why him? Why me? What is it that connects are lives so much? I can understand the blue eyes, but what about the other eight coincidences? Does it prove the theory that you come down with your whole life mapped out? Are you supposed to make the decisions you are supposed to make? Are you supposed to have the friends that you have? Do you pick your parents? If life comes at you a certain way, does it mean it's supposed to happen to you that way? If you have no control over your life, does that make every decision you make the correct decision? You just have to learn from it. Do people come down to steal, cheat, or kill? On a positive note, are people supposed to come down to volunteer, save people's lives, or win a Pulitzer? You could go crazy with all the questions. I'm sure this will give philosophers something to talk about.

My book has to be published. Is it my destiny to write my book? I wonder what he'll say when he finds out he's had part of a unique book dedicated to him. He seems like a nice guy. I wonder what publishing company will take on my book. Who will I meet in the future because of my book? What about my family in all this? How will they take my private thoughts that they don't know about? Am I putting myself in danger with the controversial subject matter? Will my book change people's lives? How will it change my life?

12/31/09.

Blue Moon happened today. Today is New Year's Eve. I don't feel like going to the party. I got through reading, *Madness: A Bipolar Life*, by Marya Hornbacher. I guess my Bipolar is not that bad.

01/02/2010.

It's the day after New Year's. I had a dream that scared me last night. I had a loaded gun in my mouth and holding a balloon. I dreamed I woke up with this stuff. The lights were not working, and I went upstairs. I saw my daughter and asked about the gun in my mouth. Then I woke for real. When I woke up from the dream the clock had 11:10pm on it. Why this number? Does it really mean 01/01/10 will be a good year?

01/15/10.

Sorry, I haven't been here for a while. I have been staying inside working on my book. I saw 11:10am on the clock today when I glanced at it. I wonder if people will take to my book like I think. Write some more query letters tomorrow.

01/30/10.

Boy, I didn't like this dream at all. It hits too close to home. I'm working one of the sectors and juggling about thirty planes, when I start forgetting frequencies to switch planes to. My hands turn cold as ice, and I can't move them. Nobody around to help me. Planes start getting very close, and I don't have control. This dream was worse than drowning dreams. I can't stand movies that have people swim underwater. I always hold my breath to see if I could've made it. I never do.

02/10/10.

I'm taking a memoirs class and got a good idea for my book title. How do you like, *Curious? An Internet Game.* It seems kind of catchy. I like the class and the instructor.

02/28/10.

I've made some nice friends in the class. They all wish me well. Nice small class.

(That is pretty much it for the old journal part.)

My Letter to Me

Hello Peggy,

It's alright, and you'll get to see another sunrise. Life as we know it can be difficult. I know the pain you had to go through. I can tell you have hope and want to find the beautiful truth. The truth is you're a wonderful person in your own individual way. Also, it's not easy to be me at times like you. Are you depressed? Don't lie to me. Would I lie to you?

Your first step is to find the correct medication and support you need for your illness. Next, comes finding out the differences between wants and needs. I can tell you have lots of love for your children, family, friends, and the world. Love actually hurts when it comes to family. Meet me halfway, and don't give up, Peggy. Everybody hurts at one time or another.

You can beat it. This will help you realize life is beautiful. If you are hurting inside, get a puzzle with a beautiful picture on it. Build the puzzle from the back side, and write words of encouragement, positive qualities, poems, and what you're thankful for. This can work for special cards too. Mail it to yourself. It gives you time to think. Put the puzzle back together with glue and put it where you can see the picture side. You will be able to turn it around so you can see the back when you want to. Then think about how you made it through the challenge of this stage in your life. You don't always have to just go with it. You are an artist of your own life. It is just that some people get paid for it. Never surrender, you have paid your dues, and now you should look forward to a life of **peace**.

PEACE
People
Energizing
Adults by
Communicating
Effectively

Everyone has challenges, which you should understand now. Love makes me wonder about life's possibilities. To find this love of yourself is part of the journey in life. Challenges are brought about by confusion.

Love,
Peggy

P.S. I'm alright. I try to always look on the bright side of life and you should try too. Life the way it is, is how you look at it. Hopefully in a positive manner. I am encouraging you with tools to make you feel better.

Jonah and the Whale

I do not believe in the story of *Jonah and the Fish*. I have seen the movie *Jaws*, based on a book by Peter Benchley, and that boat captain dies in the end. Sorry—spoiler. Jonah could not have survived in the belly of a fish, so I will make it a blue whale.

This is what the mermaids saw: While Jonah was out finding a sea monster named Krull, who lived in the dark, blue, salt waters of the coral reef, the **Wind** came along and told Jonah to help the people in one of their families, because they were having troubles. Jonah did not want to do what he was told, so the Wind gave Jonah a time-out. A blue whale named Dave, which was hanging around the coral reef, ate Jonah. Blue whales eat krill as far as I know. Anyway, Jonah stayed in the whale's stomach, and he ran out of air, then died. The whale spewed Jonah out of the blowhole. Whales do not eat people, they taste bad. People give the whales an upset stomach. When Jonah got out, he revived himself and told an incredible story of his coral reef adventure.

<u>WIND</u>

Wind moves feather.
Wind moves mountain.
Wind moves water.
Wind moves fire.
Wind moves cloud.
Wind is invisible.
Wind is variable.
Wind can embrace you.
Wind can be felt.
God is Wind.

P.S. Please keep the world's water supply clean for all living creatures. That is the naturalist in me.

Obsession

How did I become a delusional psychotic person with a mental breakdown the first time? I am sure every case is individual, but for me it was an obsessive situation. The first time was a combination of post-partum depression, caring about people's lives, and too much caffeine.

When I became "God," which was after my second child, I was obsessed with the passengers on planes. I was sure that the Air Traffic Control system was unsafe; therefore, I stayed up from dusk till dawn for three nights acting out scenarios that were safer ways of handling traffic. Also, I was talking to myself and crying. I was doing this repeatedly. Of course, postpartum depression and caffeine did not help. The racing thoughts kept me awake.

I kept calling a Federal Protection Employee Assistance help line and telling them, "I am God." They knew I needed help. My husband was away on a business trip, and luckily, we had the nanny at the time. I could not call my husband, because I was afraid, he would die on the way home. The federal employees called the police to take me to the hospital. I was telling the police that all the planes would crash that day unless they did not keep the airplanes on the ground.

When I got to the hospital with all the strangers around, I was confused and scared. This type of stuff just does not happen to me. I lived a very sheltered life, and everything always went my way. I would not take the medication they had for me, so they had to physically restrain me and give me a shot to make me sleep. Sleep deprivation caused the psychosis. They started me on several medications. This was the time when I received the medication that put me out. I did not know what the staff did to me.

With the psychotic breaks, I need to not get too obsessed about something. I need to stay on my medication, so I can stay out of the hospital. I need my sleep to stay healthy.

I used to be a working girl with the FAA. They do not let Air Traffic Controllers back to work when they have had a psychotic break. Because I loved my job so much, this led to my suicidal episode in my life. Also, what I think compounded the problem—I was not diagnosed bipolar until three years later.

Immaculate Connection

It is great to have little children. They can be a source of timeless love. It brings more challenges to one's life. I think it is *immaculate timing* when the **miracle** occurs. The part in the past, which the Bible mentions about the *immaculate birth* is hard for me to believe. They did not have In-Vitro Fertilization. Also, there were no sterile utensils around, unless I believe in an alien. Because I respect people's beliefs, I did not start this story on a big note.

I do believe that guys in the past could buy drugs from an apothecary and sexually molest a woman in her sleep who is under the influence. I believe women can blot the memory out of their minds, especially, at an early age. These scenarios can happen to men too. I have seen instances where the people hold the rape inside. I have seen that the rapists can be relatives, friends, or strangers. I know that people can conceive with mutual consent by numerous methods. This includes the scientific approach in a scientific age. Some of the situations are a subject of physical and emotional assault on females and males.

Nowadays, I have seen women have babies and keep them. I have seen women have the babies and give them up for adoption. I have seen women have abortions. I know an unexpected death of a child in or out of the womb can be a deep loss that hurts.

The choice is up to the women. What decisions will she be able to live with? I do not know everything; except I am pro-choice.

We are all immaculate at birth. I am taking the definition of born without original sin. Children are innocent at birth, but there is a point where they change. Everyone takes *a bite of the forbidden fruit*, so to speak, in life. It makes you wonder if Jesus was the outcome of rape way back when.

Final Destination

I'm calling all angels, so I can live in a field of dreams, believing this way of life can change. Some people have the ability of being able to let go of things and situations in life easier than others.

Destiny is something we attain before a final destination. To get to a final destination confusion is part of my existence. By using music, books, documentary television, nature, crafts, and journaling, I can find acceptance with obstacles. The last step is to show appreciation of people in my life. A thing should not be loved. I remember, ashes to ashes sort of thing, but hand me downs are good.

Confusion, acceptance, and appreciation add up to challenges to overcome. I cannot find everything on one-way streets. The one-way streets send me around in circles or in a square. I cannot get to a destination for progress, and *The Road Less Traveled* is a learning experience. (I am pointing out the italicized book because it is an informative book to read by M.

Scott Peck, M.D.)

Confusion on a subject or situation brings around challenges that force you to make decisions on it using the wisdom you have collected or will collect to a positive or negative outcome for yourself or someone else. You must accept the decision you have come to and show the appreciation. Appreciation can also be an understanding of the challenge and the decisions you have made and can live with. You have challenges one after another or several at one time. Everyone has a destiny. The biggest question on destiny. Why was I brought here or born? Destinies can be great or supportive. Most are supportive. You the supporters help these people be great. Without the supportive role the great cannot be. Someday just go through the day counting the decisions you must make. Do I set the clock for me to get up on time in the morning? Do I get up when it goes off or do I lay and wait for a while thinking about the day? Do I brush my teeth? What do I wear? If I decide to eat, what will it be? What time do I leave for work or appointment? How will I get to my appointment or work? These are just a fraction of daily decisions.

My life is like a puzzle. I build it, then throw it in the box of life until I need it again. Pretty baby pictures are good. Reminds me I'll be butt naked and helpless when that ashes part comes up again. I will start over again. I believe in cremation and spreading my ashes over beautiful places of my life. Just mix a little fertilizer with the old bones.

Exactly, what is a final destination? I love the word reincarnation because it has the word carnation in it. In the hereafter, I do not think you always come back as a person. I would like to come back as the majestic horse. Maybe I will get to own an Appaloosa sometime in the future.

I heard that energy does not get destroyed, and I plan to ask Einstein when I get there. One other thing, I do not want to be a human again. Been there done that, so you can't always get what you want, right.

To relax someday meet me on the equinox to watch the eclipse in a celebration by dancing with the stars for fun. Or we could borrow some space suits and take a walk on the moon.

Distractions

This never happened before to me, but I almost had a mid-air collision on my birthday at LA Center. This was my time for miracles if I ever needed one.

Here is the story: It was early *mornin'* and controllers were starting to come on shift to relieve other controllers who had worked the night shift. I took over the surveillance scope in the control room, which had the northwestern airspace, in the vicinity of Las Vegas.

One of the departures from Las Vegas was a United jet going Northwest, with an arrival flightplan to San Francisco. I cleared the jet to their requested altitude, and the pilot comes back and wishes me a "Happy Mother's Day." I replied I wasn't a mother, but it was my birthday. The United pilot comes back and wishes me a "Happy birthday."

So, here is United climbing, and I take a hand-off on a Southwest jet going the opposite direction, in conflict with United's climb.

Now, draw a horizontal line on a piece of paper going 9 o'clock to 3 o'clock. Then draw a line from 4 o'clock to 10 o'clock so that the lines intersect. That was collision point. The United jet was still climbing to an altitude above the Southwest jet. Since the air carriers were in conflict, I told United to stop at an altitude below Southwest, and then I put in a revised altitude in United's data block. This equipment is totally awesome. It informs a controller when they are about to lose separation by making the data blocks flash.

I thought *I received a read-back from United*, but I did not realize I had not succeeded in my management of the situation. I turned around to talk with another controller who was coming on duty—just being friendly. When I looked back at the scope, conflict alert was flashing between the two air carriers. United was breaking their new assigned altitude, which was supposed to be below the Southwest jet. Now, I used evasive measures to descend United immediately back down before there was a crash.

I told my supervisor I might have had an altitude bust on United. We pulled the tapes on the instructions that I had given. I found out that I was the one in error. I did not get a definite read-back from the United jet on the safe altitude. The other controller distracted me. I was just being friendly, but it could have been a deadly mistake. This was a miracle for me. There was a force looking over my shoulder on my birthday. Also, this was the best of the best birthday present ever.

I learned a lesson about not being distracted when I was managing a situation, which I was supposed to be in control.

Mayday! Mayday! Mayday!

Here is one of the thoughts, *I had in the safe house on my third time through.*

When a pilot is in distress, they call out, "Mayday! Mayday! Mayday!" that's the controller phraseology in me. They are really saying, "Help! Help! Help!" No one likes terrorism. It's, "Bad! Bad! Bad!" They kill or wound people, and they do not even stick around for the consequences. Too much blood, their stomachs cannot handle it.

Now, take the first two numbers of 9/11/01. I am sure most people got this one. That is the National Emergency number for the USA. It is a good number to call when you are suicidal, want to hurt someone, or your house is on fire—mostly in need of police, firefighters, and medical assistance.

I am going to put some doubt in about Jesus' birthday. I will come back to him again later in my book. I believe a lot of people were asking for "Help" on 9/11/01.

May 1ST is called "May Day" by most of my friends. When I was younger, we would put little cups of candy in front of friend's doors for them to find. If I put Jesus' birthday on May 1st, remember "May Day" in the month of May and "Help," in controller phraseology. Some people ask for "Help" from Jesus due to their religious beliefs. That would make Jesus have a beautiful birthday in the spring. Also, we could move Cesar Chavez Day to December 25th to celebrate since we work, live, vacation, and trade with our neighbor Mexico. That way, we can give out presents for New Year's Day. Also, might keep some drunk drivers off the roads. It is too slippery in some states.

Then May 1st would be a nice day to have Jesus' birthday and give out candy, since he was so sweet. Do I really know when Jesus was born in the time of Herod? The Bible does not say for sure.

Just a thought.

P.S. Please remember the lives lost on 9/11/01.

Destiny

It is my destiny. I believe in looking at signs and observations in life to help with decisions. Take for instance, writing my book, the word *lacuna* is so true—it was my destiny to write my book. The stories and poems came easily to me. No writer's block here. All of it came to my mind like magic. The hardest part was getting it published. What dreams may come with the publishing of my book.

Some of the bad destinies can be avoided if we look to the signs to make correct decisions. Some decisions can be deadly. The following is one true incident from Wichita Mid-Continent Airport and a rumor or urban legend from Los Angeles Center.

At Wichita Mid-Continent Airport, we would control airplanes into a small airport—within our airspace. This airport only had a VOR approach (Very High Frequency Omni-directional Range). A VOR approach is a non-precision approach because it usually uses a navigation aid not located at the airport.

Most airplanes are going to a GPS, sweet. The small airport had higher landing minimums than an ILS. The ILS is more accurate, and is found at controlled airports like Chicago, Dallas, **New York**, Philadelphia, and Phoenix. You get the idea. The ILS (Instrument Landing System) is an expensive system to install and continue to maintain. They use an ILS at busier controlled airports to get the airplanes to land safely in awfully dangerous weather, because it has lower landing minimums.

This story of a small airplane is a tragedy. This story did not happen to me, but I knew the controller who worked the airplane.

The controller was working a night shift alone, and all the airports had foggy weather. There was a small airplane that wanted to land at the small airport with a VOR approach to guide the pilot to the runway. The controller issued the bare minimums for the final approach. Some things a controller cannot control. It is like you're driving a car at night, and you hit a bicyclist that doesn't have lights or reflective equipment. It's beyond your control because of the decision of the *easy-rider*.

Well, the pilot wanted to make the approach anyway, although the controller had relayed to the pilot that they could land at Mid-Continent Airport with the ILS approach. The plane ended up going too low and hitting a power line, then immediately dove into the ground. It was a simple wrong choice that could have been avoided. These kind of situations we controllers call, *Destination-itis*. I will talk about *Destination-itis* later in the story.

This story was a rumor or urban legend that happened over thirty years ago, so I have not been able to confirm it.

A small airplane wanted to get to Utah, for a ski trip through LA Center's airspace. The controller issued a warning to the pilot that there was icing expected on his route of flight. About icing: before take-off, air carriers and large airplanes have equipment to take the ice off their airplanes. Also, they have better equipment to take the ice off during the flight.

Well, the pilot of the small airplane was given an alternate airport to land at, which did not have icing. The pilot did not take the good advice of the controller and proceeded on their route of flight. The small plane encountered the icing, which happened to be severe. The controller gave them a different altitude to escape. The pilot could not get out of the icing. The pilot called out, "Mayday! Mayday! Mayday!" All the time the controller could hear people screaming in the background. There was no way out. The airplane crashed and all were lost.

There is that *Destination-itis* again. These scenarios are within the pilots' control to make the correct decisions. *Destination-itis* is when you want to go someplace, but you have tunnel vision and are too stubborn to take the safer way. Control your own destiny for the future safety of family, friends, and fellow humans.

Why do ordinary people drive drunk in severe weather, speed during rush hour, and drive using cell phones, to mention a few things? These situations are within a human's control.

P.S. The process of fate or destiny is always on time. It is just that some people don't understand it, or they don't learn from it.

Addiction

I have not had to go through a detoxification program, but I believe there is information and help on the subject. My father, **Frank H** died of a combination of smoking, high blood pressure, diabetes, and high cholesterol. He even had to have a foot amputated.

I know some of the effect's **addictions** can have on people. Sometimes a healthy lifestyle can prevent the illness later in life. My dad's last name is **Henry**. He was in the Army and fought in the Korean and Vietnam wars. Go Veterans!

ADDICTIONS
All people
Deserve
Destinies that
Include
Carefully used
Time
In recovering from
Over used
Narcotics and
Such

"It's not that some people have willpower, and some don't. It's that some people are ready to change and others are not" (James Gordon, M.D.). I have this quotation on my kitchen counter.

P.S. I love you, and our relatives really do matter. This story was a tribute to my dad, and I am sorry if it upsets my siblings. I respected my dad. It is just that he made some wrong decisions that caught up with him in the end. Addictions can lead to depression and depression can lead to addictions.

I Have an Idea

Sorry, I cannot use dream, because that life book didn't end so well. May you rest in peace, Martin Luther King Jr.

When the Presidents take the Oath of Office, they swear on the Bible and repeat a lot of words. Some Presidents break the rules of engagement. Let us have the government stack the freedom deck in our favor. Why not swear in on a white Bible (a new beginning or silver lining representation) Bill of Rights and Constitution that govern our nation? It is up to the people to change tradition.

How about a paid, traveling Peace Team to replace our military forces? They can build more homes and **help** the hungry. This is the right stuff that makes a compassionate country.

HELP
Hello
Everyone
Let's
Partner up

The people can learn a profession they can use, and not see their friends and family die in the line of fire overseas. Why do we give a 21-gun salute to our fallen comrades? How about twenty-one carnations and a flag to the loved ones who are left behind?

Dear President Obama,

It's my life, but sometimes the government controls it. It seems to me that you have a dream and are not stuck in the lights. I know it can be rough making the difficult decisions that you have been dealt. Kind of nice knowing you like one of my relatives. So, have you ever been to Illinois? Can I come and visit sometime? Take the BBC next time and shorten the words to say.

Sincerely,
Peggy

I found a quotation by President Obama: He talks about how one voice can change a room. He encourages us to progressively use this voice to change the world (Goodreads.com).

The voice of the people makes this country so great. Let us use a little kindness to change the world. This excerpt letter is old because President Obama was elected for a second term.

Just an idea.

P.S. I do not know everything, especially how the government works. I do not want to make you mad, so I will tell you something about this story. I know the Oath of Office is short. I know we have a Peace Corps. I know we are a compassionate country. I know we are an influential nation and a leader in technology. The sentences were worded and put in here for the sake of the game. Thank you.

Control

Who has the control here? Situation: You're driving along, and you get a cell phone call or a text message. Why do you answer it? Do you want someone else to control your life? There is a time and place to be actively interested in somebody else. All concentration needs to be at hand with you. Let the cell phone call go to voicemail. You can always return the call later. Reply later for the text. If the call is an emergency, the person calling can always call 911 and get the proper assistance needed.

When I was a controller, the closest thing to being a controller was driving a car. Driving is like getting yourself in line for merging traffic. You speed up or slow down depending on the situation at hand. Also, you turn behind cars or in front of them with a safe distance in mind. Driving can be stressful and takes a lot of concentration. These are control techniques a controller must use to work air traffic in an orderly manner. Do not let the other person control your life. Be in control of your own fate or destiny. *Speedin'*, texting, or cell phone usage cause accidents. Accidents cause loss of life, property damage, and lawsuits. Why is car insurance so high? The police cannot catch all speeders or cell phone users who are driving. You think you are getting away with something. You're like a *wild-child*, so to speak, doing something wrong behind your parent's back.

Please forgive me. It is kind of hard to write in a nice voice, especially, when movies and songs are controlling my writing technique. I have done these things, and I've tried learning from my mistakes. Luckily, I did not get involved in a serious accident.

I have driven home so drunk that I had to drive cross-eyed to see straight. I should have taken a taxi home. Getting *wasted* or *stoned* on illegal drugs I have done. I've driven home nodding off behind the wheel. I have gotten moving violations. I have driven with the cell phone in my hand. (Driving and cell phone usage is illegal in California now, but I still see people doing it.) With these situations, the victim's life is taken too soon—possibly yours. I am trying to persuade you to take control of your life.

I'm in control, then again, I'm not. What is going on that can control your life and others?

Lucky

Why do people *hang-around*, so to speak, famous people like a flock of seagulls? It seems that the famous people are trying to wave the seagulls off, but the seagulls are too stubborn to take to flight. Remember back when I was an Air Traffic Controller, and I could ride up front with the pilots? Good.

Here is the story: I was waiting for a certain flight out of Los Angeles Airport, when a famous performer came to get on the flight. Well, people who were not a relative or real friend would come up to this person for their signature or photograph during their personal time.

I think we have enough germs to worry about. I am sure the seagulls didn't use sanitizer first. While I was sitting without an invasion of privacy, I am thinking, *I was lucky to see this person.* Also, who had the more important job here? To act like an Air Traffic Controller in a movie is nothing like being one. Movies are partly shown on location for reality purposes. Basically, it makes the scenes as real as possible. For instance, the movies *Always* and *Close Encounters of the Third Kind* had location shots. You do not get the real idea of what it's like to be a controller. There are on-site film shots with movies. The next time you see a famous person that is in the spotlight, just think of the food chain. It all starts at the bottom and works its way up. Everybody's job is important for the world to go around in an organized manner. Hollywoodland makes movies about your job too. You know they don't know what it's really like. Oh, I take that back. A lot of famous people worked their way up with jobs like we do. I used to work at a factory job that helped to produce electricity. Who needs electricity?

On with the "Lucky" story. I'm riding up with the pilots when I must use the restroom. There was this person sitting up in first class. Nice, I can see why they do it. They can afford the comfort and privacy to some degree.

When I came out of the unisex bathroom, the famous person strikes up a conversation. I didn't initiate the action. We started to talk about jobs. They asked me why I was up front with the pilots, and I told them why. I got the usual response, "It must be a stressful job." I smiled and said, "Yes." I'd like to include that police and firefighter's have a stressful job, because they put their lives on the line daily. I loved the adrenaline rush of being a controller. Controllers are not as responsible for crashes, as much as equipment malfunctions, weather, war, or pilot error just to mention a few examples.

Now, this famous person had a little bit of a bad reputation. This person was nice once you got to know them. Don't even try to pull this person out of me. The secret is going to my blowing ashes. The famous people can make mistakes and learn from them and move on with life's challenges.

Whisper after me. *People are only people*, so read a book, pay attention to your own family, or play with your computer using my book. You will find these people being normal with sunglasses, no make-up, sweats, jeans, t-shirts, and caps.

Fred Allen was a popular comedian radio host of *The Fred Allen Show*. He mentions how a celebrity will go to ways of hiding themselves after they become famous (Brainyquote.com).

Look at them when they shine like stars across the universe. Why hasn't man landed on a star up high? The bright star is too hot, far, and away. Do not touch though, you might make them go supernova. Just consider yourself lucky that you were able to see some stardust up close.

I remember the controller sitting next to Holly Hunter in the movie, *Always*, that lucky guy.

With or Without You

Dear John,

My letter is for your eyes only. All of me is what I want to give you. The face of love is what you will see in me. There is always something to remind me about you. Just give me a reason to be brave. It's all about love in my letter to you. John, you are my soulmate. I want to make you feel my love, so here is the struggle I have daily when it comes to you.

You see, if I had you all to myself, we would make a perfect love in my eyes. We are young still, so there is time for us to be together. I'm watching you constantly, and given the chance, I would give you an American Beauty Rose. This has been a good year for you, and you have a beautiful mind that sets you apart from all the rest. Someone like you is a drug that I just can't get enough of, and it seems like I can say anything to you. Nobody knows the thoughts I have about you, so I will never say never when it comes to you and I. I do have to say, I confessed to Constantine, the priest, over my obsession with you. You are notorious for using the perfect combination in creativity and life.

John, I know your career keeps us apart, but I accept this. Please do not let me down with my love for you, but I know you will at times, and I accept that too. Say something and this letter is to tell you my foolish heart beats fast when I see you. You make me feel like there is always sunshine in my life. All I want is you. Without you, I'm lost in a sea of despair, but I know that I will survive, so I can see you again. You know I won't go home without you, but you push me away until I do. I know you try to find another but let her go. I'm all you need. Just a kiss from you would make my actions justified to need you now in my life. I will always love you, and I want to be the only person in your eyes. It's not only that, but I can't take my eyes off you when I see you.

I cannot tell you how many mirrors I have cracked, because I could not see your reflection in them. If tomorrow doesn't come with you, I know I will love you forever from a distance. Love me or leave me, it would be your choice. If you leave, I will have to love you from afar. I look to the leprechaun with his pot of gold to help me out with my wish for you to be by my side always. The faster I run to you makes me realize I'm not over you. I'm dreaming of you day and night.

Also, I don't stop dreaming about you, because that's just the way I am. I know I go crazy over you, but I can't help it. John, I have written a love story where you are mine, so if we were together, what would our favorite song be? I hope you dance with me and the melody will come. Something about you could easily make me put a revolver to my head if I can't have you.

The prophecy is clear in my eyes. Let me in because I've loved you so long. Sometimes I think me before you, but the red lights I see makes me stop thinking this way. Don't make me stop *lovin'* you. The proposal from me is for us to make a pretty baby together. What if I found someone else? Would you be jealous? Nobody but me could love you. I'm *runnin'* to you because I *wanna* be the one. Hold on you say, love yourself first, but I beg for mercy. There is the hunger in me with every breath you take. I love you. There I said it.

John, I got this. I would climb a mountain to get to the fields of open flowers that remind me of you. I know I don't play by the rules, because that is just the way it is. I want your kiss and tell me to hold on to you. A change is *gonna* come where you don't run away. It's just not black or white and you know me better than I know myself. I just can't let you go another lonely night without me. The light falls away but we never close our eyes. Listen, all I ask is for you to listen. My heart will go on. I just have to have a little faith. "F" is for family and you say, "What's the game plan?" The game plan is I'll be the stalker and you will be the prey. Just love me tender or give me some tender loving care thrown my way.

John, this is my heart crying out for you, so don't kiss me goodbye. With my love sometimes I must let it go. The blind side of me is where you come from, so it is easy for you to knock me off my feet. For the first time, I saw the light, and it is you. I have several qualities that would keep me by your side. Stand by me, and we could conquer the world. I've been loving you too long. I spy on you, but you don't see me. I'm in no rush, but you belong with me, so stay the night. If I stay, would you go my way? This is it for now until I write again.

All my love,
The Fan

Hello all, this letter is an example of how a person can get caught up in the life of another person with delusional aspects. Do not let it happen to you. Keep your admiring eyes on the internet and keep your distance. You are not these famous people's soulmate. Live your life and let them have theirs.

Lost in Translation?

I had a quotation by Nostradamus in here. He mentions how people give up a part of themselves when they are deceitful (Goodreads.com).

This is my translation of his quotation, but it might not make any sense.

We give our gifts to the lie, for it is in our nature to cheat, and when we lie, we give our gifts.

Think of it, everyone is born with choice, intelligence, and the gift of life. When we die they will be gone but hopefully not forgotten.

Here are some questions I have. When does intelligence turn into wisdom? Does wisdom affect our choices? Who has control over a life to determine if it will be short or long? Who really knows how to understand Nostradamus? Do you get what you give in life? How do you know?

I want to talk about deceitful people. Scammers and hackers are a big thing now. There are companies getting hacked and held for ransom. I have given away four-thousand dollars to scammers. Remember if it is too good to be true it is probably a scam. If you have children or relatives that can help, ask them about the situation. Research on the internet.

What I Have Learned

This process will grow as I figure out the purpose of my *so-called* life. I did figure out a lot on my last stay at the hospital.

A. I know I will not always look at obstacles as *half-full*, but I try.

B. I know that exercising, seeking knowledge, and eating healthy is good.

C. I know caffeine, drugs, or alcohol affect my mind, body, and spirit. I choose not to give in.

D. I do not have to be around negative, aggressive, controlling, hurtful, and condescending people. I choose not to associate with them, but I will tolerate them if I cannot leave. It is up to them to change, not me.

"Arrogance is having high self-confidence to a level where you become narcissistic. You feel like you're better than everyone else in every area. You minimize the opinion of other people and abilities by making them feel inferior compared to you" (Angie Murillo).

I learn more with positive conversations on a 1 to 1 or 2 to 1 basis with people who are friendly and open minded.

E. I strive to get along with new people because I know how to be considerate. New people might look to be part of a crowd and make new connections that are positive. Some people are uncomfortable standing out, so I help to bring them in. Some people like their solitude, and I respect that trait. Think of a herd of zebras or antelope. They stay together for security and socializing. The predators seek out the weak and sick. *I choose not to join the lion's pride*, so to speak. I believe people communicate passively, assertively, or passionately. Anyone of these traits can be done excessively, so there needs to be moderation.

F. I know I have the right to seek the proper training, therapy, and medicine for the challenges in my life. I have chosen the correct doctors for my situations. They should bee around longer than me. They make honey, but sometimes they must sting to get my attention. I used a homophone.

G. I am an almost peaceful and patient person, and I'm not a threat to others.

H. All people have choices, and I respect their decisions. I personally do not carry 21 guns, or as a matter of fact, no guns at all. Personal choices are hardest to understand.

I. I strive to stay happy and calm, so I do not *teeter-totter up and down*, so to speak. I am only human. I do not want to *fall down the rabbit hole*. It is too confusing.

J. I was suicidal at one time, and I have forgiven myself. I am glad I didn't succeed. I have survived probably one of the biggest challenges in my life so far.

K. I choose to live a life of challenges that end in success. Success does not always happen in golf, sometimes, the ball gets lost in the water.

L. I choose to live a life of family and friends. I love them very much. I care about other people.

M. I am here to learn from my mistakes and challenges in life. I look to the **future**.

FUTURE
Fantastic
Under
The
Universe;
Right
Earth

I Believe

I know some of the stories I write can be touchy, but it is that scientific and caring side of me most of the time. This can be a frustrating part of me. I did not get what I wanted today and that was to go home and be with my children, so I'm taking it off my shoulders. I want to see my life as *half-full* again and not *half-empty*. Maybe **Perceval** can bring me the Grail, **to battle this war and turn it into peace**. These are my frustrated thoughts.

I believe Jesus was kind and gentle. He might have been killed for being a homosexual, different color, religion, or his beliefs that he could bring peace for all people.

I believe there is a force that can control my *half-empty* and *half-full* spirit of my soul.

I believe I can find hope and thankfulness this time in knowledge, music, ping-pong, wonder, nature, friends, and journaling. There are forces that are negative that I must use the power of now to let go.

Are all these statements untrue to me? No, I know what I have experienced and follow my heart to the best of my abilities. I know I am respectful of other people's beliefs. It is hard for me to believe that Jesus could do what he did by rumors, myths, or legends.

I believe some people will believe my realizations to be true or untrue depending on their beliefs. I know I will continue to research and find the truth in all I do by seeking knowledge on subjects that interest me.

I believe in ghosts or spirits, but I do not put them on a pedestal. They can go through me or scare me. I can find the healing aspect of others and myself in the beliefs that we will get better.

I know I want the *computer of my mind*, so to speak, to grow.

I believe in giving money and time to family, friends, and charities within my control. I do not do this excessively.

I know I will not try to change other people's beliefs, but I hope they will succeed in providing peace in the world by common laws that govern their countries, states, and communities. I know these are my thoughts on sensitive subjects, but I could not hesitate any longer.

I believe some people will boycott and speak out against my beliefs in a critic's type of way. I do not know if people will pass my book on as a learning tool, myth, or legend type of way.

I remember the fictional book, *Fahrenheit 451,* by Ray Bradbury that was made into a movie. The plot is that some people did not like nice people learning stories and knowledge passed down in books, so the *know-it-all people* burned the valuable books for their own purposes. These actions upset the people who wanted to learn and enjoy the stories from the books. The people who wanted to learn would memorize the books from generation to generation. What I do not know is, as time went by, whether the good people would leave parts of the story out, or add information because they were only human, like me.

I waited till the end of my stories to put my thoughts to paper, so I would not forget the incident that brought this writing around.

I believe Jesus in the Bible was like any other person who wanted to love, but he did not get what he wanted. He still wanted peace and happiness, but before he could, others killed him in the prime of his life. He did not get what most people want, and that is to live.

It is not in my human nature to change other people's minds, but to have them look at the coincidences that make them think about a person or meet a person, about something we don't know or understand. Some people tell me of situations they have experienced, but I do not take them all as truth.

Nostradamus, a French apothecary, and seer believed that some people are deceitful. I am glad for people and myself if we try to prove him wrong. I want to follow my loving heart and apply it to my hopefully peaceful life.

I believe some people hurt other people and defenseless animals, steal, cheat, and deceive in one way or another; even though, they know it is wrong. I do not know if these deceitful people will change, but I hope they will.

I do not know if people will take the stories in my book as true. Some of the stories are lighthearted in a funny sort of way. Poems can be stories. I think some of the stories can be serious. I do not know everything, because I'm an average person and have not seen it all.

I do get to see lovely and not so lovely pictures on the internet, newspaper, books, television, and nature. I know there is knowledge in some of the information for me.

I see violence everywhere. The violent part of life depresses me, so I listen to upbeat **music** that speaks to the individual in me. Do you think life would be senseless without music?

MUSIC
Muse
Under
Success
Includes
Calmness

I love quotations because I love some of the messages in them. I look up the author and find out more about them. It is like going to the end of a book for the punchline.

Henry D. Thoreau comments on how people go through life walking to different rhythms, and we should accept that (Brainyquote.com).

Henry D. Thoreau, I think, was a complicated person of a peaceful nature. Seneca, a Roman philosopher, and statesman killed himself because an official told him to do it.

I believe terrorists nowadays kill themselves, and innocent people, to make people change their minds to the terrorist's beliefs. I do not think it is right. It breaks the universal law of no killing in the world.

I believe the government of the USA has spread itself too thin. The deficit in the nation proves this statement.

I believe that there are successful people who share a lot of their earnings and time because of their struggles in the past. I love volunteers and givers of monetary value to the less fortunate and animal care.

I believe that the middleman can take advantage of the people who pay for their services.

I believe there can be peace in a time of strife in the world.

I believe two children or less for all couples in today's economy. There just is not enough to go around.

In some animals, it is in their nature to attack for a living, but all are getting to the point of extinction.

I hope people will conserve life and energy to the best of their abilities.

I wrote this story because of the things I see in the world and in the past.

I am happy now because of the facility auction. Generous people donate new items and clothes. It makes people happy in a fun way in a schedule that is a *hard pill to swallow*, so to speak. Also, donations to the ill can uplift their spirits. Now I see the *half-full* part of my life. I'm yours journal and you gave my life direction.

Thank you.

Viggo Mortensen mentions how we should be **curious** to get to know each other. You just need to get together peacefully to consider each other's ideas and realize you might think the same (Brainyquote. com).

CURIOUS
Cause
Under
Right decisions
Include
Outcomes that
Unite
Souls

Communication in a non-confrontational manner promotes learning.

On Writing

These are my paraphrasing renditions on quotations that you might be able to find on the internet. I am being vague. They all have something to do with writing. I can learn a lot from quotations on life.

Theodore Isaac Rubin believes that by writing a book you can change, and it does not matter if the book sells or not (Greatthoughtstreasury.com).

A Marshall McLuhan quotation I was able to find had to do with giving information on yourself that can be an invasion of privacy (Brainyquote.com).

To me Stephen King is a great writer. He mentions how it can bring you back to reality (Goodreads.com).

My writing technique mirrors something said by Francois-René de Chateaubriand, that I am original, and no one will be able to copy me (Goodreads.com).

One of Horace's statements has to do with the reader. You can teach something along the way by keeping their interest (Thinkexist.com).

Finally, Ralph Waldo Emerson talks about how everyone loves a quote (Goodreads.com).

Poems

I've put some child-type poems in my book.

<u>Practical Magic</u>
My magic will work.
I know it will.
I know it will.
I know it will.
Third time is a charm. Why?
Because, I said so.

———⊂∞⊃———

TESTS of TIME
Truth is within my grasp.
Eat healthy and exercise, so I
Stay on the right track.
Together I stand, so I
Survive the Tests of Time.
of (with)
Togetherness
In
Messages I
Evolve

———

Very Best
As I do my very best,
Can you understand my quest?
How the time goes away so fast,
I'm the one who faces my past.
Life is short at least for me,
Helps me learn to love you see.
This will take my soul I know,
From the time I saw first snow.
From the start it comes from heart,
While I carve my name on bark.
The clocks in time tell me there's time to play.
In my place do I go or stay?
Can you understand my quest?
As I do my very best.

———

Beds

Alley oop here's the scoop,
A bedtime rhyme for you.
In the shed you'll find your beds,
As cozy as can be.
But *lo and behold* it's trunks for bunks,
Your eyes can trick you see.
Half asleep you fumble and mumble,
Just watch out for the tumble!

Beauty

The beauty I like,
Catches my eyes in the morning light.
Vivid flowers, bright sunlight, vibrant birds,
All were resting last night.
Beauty this morning relies on my sight.

Danielle

Danielle's nice,
But adds a little spice.
With light blue eyes,
That matches the skies.
Purple and Pink,
Us Pinzon's think…
2
Is a wonderful year!

Just for You

Rumbly, tumbly, wobbly-woo,
I have a baby just for you.
Lovie, dovie, titty-tat,
Who would have imagined that?

—— ◦◦◦ ——

Kitten Kitten

Kitten Kitten eyes so new.
When you grow up will they be yellow, green, or blue?
Kitten Kitten eyes for sight.
What will they look at in day or night?
Kitten Kitten eyes that talk.
What will they say when you play or walk?
Kitten Kitten you'll be a cat soon.
Let me hold you forever and a moon.

—— ◦◦◦ ——

Purring

Cat purring on my feet; so sweet.
Cleaning, licking; what keeps him ticking?
Playing with my pencil; so simple.
Black as night; with no fright.
My companion for the night.
Piece of string; such a thing.
Luckily he doesn't have wings.

—— ◦◦◦ ——

Curious

Curious cat where you at?
Under the chair…why there?
On the car…how far?
In the garden…beg your pardon.
Over the fence…makes me wince.
Up the tree…quite free.
Through the pipe…*yipe*!
Over my shoulder…couldn't be bolder.
How curious you are to me.

My Kindergartner

A child I would send,
In girl's clothing to mend.
Memories she brought home,
I relayed on the phone.
At the end of the year,
A first grader I cheered!
A child I would pull,
A boy not wanting school.
His pockets full of stones,
I'm avoiding the phones.
At the end of the year,
My vacation is near!
With a family of four,
We have fun galore.
When summer is done,
Its school we've won!
All children with wonder,
School after summer.
I think teachers are cool,
I'll supply some tools!

Starlight

Stars up high,
That makes me sigh.
Brilliant as diamonds in the sky.
Silent with nothing to say,
Beautiful as a day in May.
A light for me to stay,
To blind me as a sunny day.
Grouped in the Milky Way,
Hits me like a ray.
I do not have to pay.
It's hard for me to say good-bye,
When daylight shines high.

———ထဆာ———

Midnight Love

Midnight walk,
Love to talk.
Holding hands,
That is grand.
I might stumble,
It makes him mumble.
No trouble here.
It makes him Dear.

Don't let your mind wander so much.
Bad girl! Bad girl!
Think up poems instead. OK! OK!

One Poem that's all. What do I do now?
Do more **poems**.
I can't stop reading "Midnight Love!"

———ထဆာ———

Lightning

Lightning shining bright by knight.
Flashing for the evening sight.
Clapping follows the brightest light.
Knight to knight tonight.
Tonight for light for light.
Will you stay for me tonight?

―――⸰―――

The Starry Night

The starry night with bright moonlight.
The stars are shining instead of whining.
The moon is glowing for the sake of showing.
A beautiful time to fly.
With all stars shining,
I could be mining.
The moon is up in the sky,
Brilliant as a **pearl** on high.

―――⸰―――

PEARL

Peace
Enlightens
All
Righteous
Lives

"Pearl" is the meaning of my name. I had to stick that one in.

―――⸰―――

Hummingbird

I'm a Hummingbird, so let me out the door.
I'm a male. I need daylight to explore.
My wings are made for flight,
But can't hum at night.
My feathers colorful to the eyes,
That helps reflect the beautiful skies.
I eat the nectar of a flower,
But never when it showers.
My heart beats fast,
And strong when it lasts.
My lifespan is long you see,
For me to make the Harmony.

My Cat

My cat is black as night.
His eyes reflect the light.
He prowls around without a sound,
And then cannot be found.

Dedicated to Blackjack

Creativity
Comes from the:
Brain
Body
Heart
Soul

———∞∞∞———

My Stuffed Animal
Be it a:
Soft kitten that I was so smitten.
Smelly bear that was always there.
Scruffy puppy that was so lovely.
Green frog that helped me sleep like a log.
Silly monkey that made me think of something funky.
Wild pony that I called Tony.
Tiny mouse that was big as a house.
Busy rabbit that became my habit.
Rough dinosaur that was quite an eyesore.
The wolf that made me cool.
You had ears and eyes so big with understanding,
Because I was so very demanding.
You took some load off Mom and Dad,
Which I'm sure made them very glad.
My stuffed animal you see was a lot like me.

———∞∞∞———

Circle of Friends
His and Her circle of friends,
To rule the mall.
His and Her circle of friends,
To find the mall.
His and Her circle of friends,
They bring to the mall.
And in the darkness dwell at the mall.

Memories
Giraffes are called graceful and tall.
Kelly we blend elegance and friend.
You and I together memories forever.

Flamingos our name, soccer the game.
Camryn played with heart from the very start.
You and I together memories forever.

Sundevils' our name, volleyball the game.
Lauren would always start and played the part.
You and I together memories forever.

Otters are called playful and smart.
Tyler and I are never apart.
You and I together memories forever.

Heart

An envelope filled with love,
And stolen kisses sent from above.
They landed on my cheek, now yours,
Giving you the key to a door.
A very special door indeed,
One that will never lock and keep us apart.
The door that leads to my Heart.

Light/Night

The butterfly beautiful to my sight.
You are a creature of the Light.
The butterfly in Light flies toward the Night.
Why do you take to flight?
Because you lay still at Night.

The moth is fluffy to my sight.
You are a creature of the Night.
The moth at Night flies toward the Light.
Why do you take to flight?
Because you're blinded by the Light.

<u>Eternity</u>
Illumination is the Path.
Rendezvous is the Beginning.
Patience is the Journey.
Heredity is the Revelation.
Imagination is the Inspiration.
Dapper is the Style.
Courage is the Hero.
Serendipity is the seconds of Time.
Sublime is the Life.
Edification is the Thought.
Love is the Passion.
Foreplay is the Fantasy.
Climax is the Ecstasy.
Eden is the Paradise.
Experience is the Wisdom.
Euphoria is the Destination.
Celestial is Me.

Precious

Precious is like:
A Flower beautiful to the Eye.
Nature that always takes my Breath away.
Health to live a long Life.
The Taste of the Mist.
To Hear an Ocean lapping against the shore.
A Light which Blinds me.
A Soul that returns to Heaven.
Salvation that takes my Sins away.
Time and Wonder.

<u>Only Time Will Tell</u>

Where am I going?
Why do I feel this way?
Who can help me?
What can I do?
Only Time Will Tell.

How do I know?
When is the time right?
When will we find each other?
Heart of my soul.
Only Time Will Tell.

Together as one.
Up in the day, then into the night.
Holding, touching, feeling, seeing:
Us forever.
Only Time Will Tell.

Life
Life is like value,
White to black to white.
Life is like water,
Clear to dirty to clear.
Life is like a flower,
Seed to flower to seed.
Life is like a child,
Light to adult to light.
What is the meaning of life?
You know you just forgot.

Love Story

I go nowhere but end up somewhere by your side.
When I get there, I'm amazed at what I find.
It's the love for you that makes me want to confide.
Our love rolls in like the waves of a tide.
Like the stars throughout the universe which makes it wide.
Do we take our time for the long stride?
My quick love for you makes me blind.
I'm crazy for you to be my beautiful bride.
For a marriage story I look for us to be twined.
It's the key that will make us bind.
The children we have will give us pride.
We will make sure we are their guide.
This is what I see in my mind.
Together for life is what I've eyed.
A love story for all time.

Anticipation

The mystery of not knowing.
The temptation of the mystery.
The redemption of the temptation.
The imagination of the redemption.
The enthusiasm of the imagination.
The confrontation of the enthusiasm.
The excitement of the confrontation.
The illumination of the excitement.
The revelation of the illumination.
The rendezvous of the revelation.
The patience of the rendezvous.
The affordability of the patience.
The uncertainty of the affordability.
The contemplation of the uncertainty.
The residence of the contemplation.
The principle of the residence.
The righteousness of the principle.
The fantasy of the righteousness.
The end of anticipation.

The Quatrain

An honor will be bestowed,
Never before in history.
The prominent people will send,
For answers they intend.

My soulmate who hides,
Will begin to seek.
The answers are in my book,
All he needs to do is look.

With a song in my head,
And a soul in my heart.
I've given my tooth to a fairy,
To make my life merry.

Good-Bye

I don't want to say good-bye. Maybe in the future I'll come back, so I will leave you with these messages. The blank pages in the back are for your creative **ideas** or list the movies and songs that you could find.

Hallelujah! Someday say Hey! Soul Sister to me.

<u>IDEAS</u>
It deserves
Everyone's
Attention
SALVATION! Have you said your prayers today?

This is where I had a quotation by St. Francis of Assisi. It is part of a prayer, I think. It has to do with how a person can cause peace by using love to overcome hatred. It is on a bracelet I own. I am sure you can find it on some website. I probably could have put it in under fair use, but I did not want to take any chances.

Sincerely,
"Deborah the Prophetess"

P.S. This was my last delusional episode when I went into the hospital on 08/20/09. Salvation is about forgiving yourself then changing for the better. *We can all be butterflies*, so to speak. Can we all strive for *simple minds*? Take the last sentence as we can become stress free.

Cheats

Whataya want from me? Oh yeah, the cheats. To help you there are songs inside of songs, songs inside of movies, movies inside of movies, and songs that are movies. These are what I found, but there could be more. I highly doubt it though. Do not forget the numbers and grouping words together. Look at story and poem titles. Some of the movies inside of movies went something like this: I would put in the word "Blank," then that movie would pop up plus the movie, "The Blank." I counted them as two movies since they were different movies all together. That is what was so great about Netflix. It gave you several movies to choose from. There were movies and songs with the same titles, but I only counted the ones that had the more popular artists or recent dates of release. Due to repeating of words, one song or movie can be found in several stories or poems.

I am going to give you some hints on one of the movies. The movie is a two-lettered word, and it is a very common word and in several stories. It started out as a book and was made into a movie. Because there is a clue in the "On Writing" page, I am sending you there specifically.

So, have fun looking up your favorite artists that you enjoy on the internet like I did.

Good Night and Good Luck.

Introduction: 0
Dedications: 2 songs
Names: 2 songs
Shawls: 3 songs, 2 art
Quotations: 4 art
The Fun Part: 12 songs, 36 art
Nothing but the Truth: 28 songs, 94 art, and **7 clues**
Wolfie: 6 songs, 16 art
Body is not Symmetrical: 7 songs, 20 art, and **2 clues**
Eve and Adam: 17 songs, 69 art, and **1 clue**
Snowball just HIT me: 3 songs, 10 art, and **2 clues**
Art: 2 songs, 10 art, and **five clues**
Thankful: 4 songs, 13 art
Mother Nature is Hurting: 7 songs, 30 art
Survivors vs. Losses: 5 songs, 12 art
My Journal: 33 songs, 110 art, and **3 clues**
My Letter to Me: 19 songs, 12 art
Jonah and the Whale: 4 songs, 10 art
Obsession: 2 songs, 11 art

Immaculate Connection: 1 song, 10 art, and **1 clue**
Final Destination: 7 songs, 20 art
Distractions: 7 songs, 15 art
Mayday! Mayday! Mayday!: 2 songs, 3 art
Destiny: 5 songs, 23 art, and **1 clue**
Addiction: 3 songs, 4 art, and **2 clues**
I Have an Idea: 6 songs, 11 art
Control: 9 songs, 18 art
Lucky: 11 songs, 13 art
With or Without You: 93 songs, 60 art
Lost in Translation?: 1 song, 7 art
What I Have Learned: 7 songs, 19 art
I Believe: 5 songs, 19 art, and **4 clues**
On Writing: 4 art
Practical Magic: 3 art
Tests of Time: 1 art
Very Best: 3 songs, 5 art
Beds: 1 song, 2 art
Beauty: 2 art
Danielle: 0
Just for You: 0
Kitten Kitten: 1 song, 1 art
Purring: 2 art
Curious: 3 art
My Kindergartener: 7 art
Starlight: 2 songs, 4 art
Midnight Love: 1 song, 2 art, and **1 clue**
Lightning: 0

The Starry Night: 1 song, 2 art, and **1 clue**
Hummingbird: 1 song, 1 art
My Cat: 0
Creativity: 0
My Stuffed Animal: 2 art, **1 clue**
Circle of Friends: 1 art
Memories: 1 song, 1 art
Heart: 3 art
Light/Night: 2 art
Eternity: 7 songs, 13 art
Precious: 1 song, 5 art
Only Time Will Tell: 2 songs, 1 art
Life: 1 song, 3 art
Love Story: 2 art
Anticipation: 0
The Quatrain: 1 song, 2 art
Good-Bye: 3 songs, 5 art
Cheats: 1 song, 7 art
Circle O: 3 songs, 8 art

Circle O

My circle of friends that we have in common, that's what I like about you.

Double Diamond
Green Eyes
Best Friends
Rock and Roll Guy
Bee
Whoopi Goldberg
Grace
Keanu Reeves
Dear
Nicole Kidman
Angel
Winning
Pure Hearted
Neil Diamond
Famous Warrior
The Brave One

Juliette Lewis
DTM
Barbra Streisand
"White Cloud"
Nice Nurses
Emerald Eyes
Bible Man
May
Famed
The Lucky One

Again, I have not met the actors and actresses mentioned. People just look like them. They do not endorse my book.

Ideas

_____
_____
_____
_____
_____
_____
_____
_____
_____
_____
_____
_____
_____
_____
_____
_____
_____
_____
_____
_____

_____

_____

_____

_____

_____

_____

_____

_____

_____

_____

_____

_____

_____

_____

_____

_____

_____

_____

_____

_____

_____

_____

_____

_____

CPSIA information can be obtained
at www.ICGtesting.com
Printed in the USA
JSHW010933220822
29544JS00005B/12